Running Life's Marathon

Running Life's Marathon

A Practical Commentary on the Letter to the Hebrews

Paul Wakely

Contents

Foreword

I am so pleased that Paul agreed to my invitation to lead a few days of concentrated bible study on the book of Hebrews. There is so much deep insight flowing through his veins concerning the word of God, and this opportunity opened a window for us to look through and wonder at what we saw. But we were determined that this would not just be an intellectual exercise: we wanted the participants to encounter something of the reality of what they were reading and hearing about. Setting the days' gatherings in the context of worship, this is what happened over the course of that week, and now that these sessions are available here in written form, my hope is that the same would happen for a wider audience: to know, deeply, more of the wonder of Jesus and what he has done for us.

I have known Paul closely as a friend since 1987 and we have shared hours together fellowshipping over so many aspects of life, family, ministry and especially the word of God. Paul loves the word of God, comprehending it not just academically, but reading every page with a view to finding its deeper meaning, a revelation of the Father and Jesus. I think Paul understands, more than most, that the central message of the gospel is an invitation into an eternal relationship with the Father and the Son and the Holy Spirit. These pages will draw you into the divine dance, all made possible through the cross.

The bible is an unfolding revelation of the heart of God. The book of Hebrews helps us to understand that the Old Testament all points to Jesus and that everything we need is made known to us through his birth, life, teaching, death and resurrection. Jesus is the substance of the shadow and opens the door of grace for us all to walk through.

In this study Paul beautifully takes us by the hand and leads us into an understanding of the true magnificence of Jesus. Take the journey and let your heart fall deeper and deeper in love with Jesus.

Clive Jackson
Founding Pastor, Father's House, Shaftesbury, UK

Introduction

Overview of the letter to the Hebrews

The book of the letter to the Hebrews is a rich treasure trove. I have called this journey through it 'Running Life's Marathon,' because as we travel through the letter, I believe it will be a guide and encouragement to us in our own race. Our hearts will burn more and more with faith and confidence, enabling us to continue all the way to the finish line with our last breath. I trust that as we engage with this text, each one of us will be caught up in a tangible encounter, where the anointing on this word opens up divine revelation to our hearts, bringing not just understanding in our minds but also hope to our spirits. If we can approach it with an openness to anything God might want to say to us, we are in for an exciting journey!

The foundational approach here is that, 'All scripture is God-breathed' (2 Tim 3:16). In our day it is contested that *all* scripture is God-breathed, so I am stating clearly my starting point, that every single part of the scriptures, from start to finish, is divinely inspired. The Holy Spirit brought it to us from heaven, it comes from the Lord and it is not partly of God and partly man-made. It is indeed 'useful for instruction, for conviction, for correction, and for training in righteousness.' The book of Hebrews is useful for instructing, rebuking, encouraging and inspiring our hearts, every bit of it, and because of that it is important that we position ourselves 'under' it rather than stand over it and say, 'I don't like that, I'm not sure it really says that.' We should, rather, come under its authority with an attitude that says, 'God breathed this into me, so that my journey might be richer.' There may be all sorts of questions that come up for us in this journey, and it is quite acceptable to disagree with another's interpretation, but we cannot try to make scripture say what it doesn't say, or to say something that would make things easier for us, or what we think it should say.

Who is it written to? To Jewish believers, to Christians from a Jewish background, and therefore there are a lot of references in the book to the Old Testament, the Old Covenant, and all the practices surrounding that. It was probably written to a group of churches in one area, possibly in Jerusalem or Judea, or in Rome. When was it written? This is unknown, but it was probably in the late 60s AD. The clues are found in chapters 2:3 and in 10:32-34 where the writer is obviously talking to second generation believers who had heard the gospel from those who actually knew Jesus, describing persecution they had already suffered. There is also no mention of the destruction of Jerusalem in AD 70. Most commentaries therefore date it somewhere around the late 60s AD.

Who wrote it? There are several possible suggestions: for many centuries Paul was considered to be the letter's author, but the stylistic differences from his other writings made that thought to be unlikely. Two of the other candidates who have been considered are Barnabas, who was an intellectual Hebrew believer, well-versed in the Old Testament, and Apollos, another Jewish believer, a learned man with a thorough knowledge of the scriptures. It may be one of these who wrote this letter, but we simply do not know.

This background context is really helpful in understanding the detail of the text. The Jews venerated the Old Covenant with its institutions of the Law, the temple, the sacrifices and offerings, and the priesthood. Have you ever been to a country where the culture and practices completely puzzle you until you understand the history of the people you are amongst? I remember that the first two times I went to the Philippines, I could not understand so much of their culture, both spiritually and in terms of their normal social practices. I could not understand why they appeared to be so subservient all the time, until I understood their history, that they had been constantly invaded and overtaken by other nations to such a degree that many of them had taken on something of a slave mentality, rather than expressing the dignity of who they really were as a nation.

When I understood that history, I understood that their culture and ways and even their spirituality had become distorted, so they were less able to understand that God could be a loving Father to them.

Unless we understand the journey of the Jews and how deeply they venerated the Old Covenant, with all the practices, sacrifices, offerings and so on, where the High Priest could only come before God once a year (and then in fear and trembling), we will not understand the huge transformation the New Covenant brings. This veneration of the old hardened the great body of the Jewish people against the gospel, with its promise to completely replace the Old Covenant. In other words, we need to understand what a shock it was to the Jews to hear 'I'm sorry brothers, all of that is over now.' We have to understand how deeply they had guarded it and held onto it, believing there is only one true God, worshipping him, and connecting with him through the Old Testament scriptures, the covenant, the sacrifices. This is the way they connected with him, in the limited way they did, but then suddenly they were being told, 'all that is over, it is finished.' Because of that veneration, they struggled to change their mindsets towards that of the New Covenant, and they kept looking back to the old. The writer to the Hebrews is constantly reminding them that they must understand the connection between the two but also the conclusion of the whole old system, to make way for the new and better things.

Many born-again Jews were heavily influenced by keeping to external practices belonging to the Old Covenant, mediated by Moses. The question then arises, did some early believers in Christ still hold to practices, religious duties, ways of behaving, or a distorted reliance on aspects of Jewishness that had nothing to do with the wonderful covenant won through Jesus' blood? And then we should ask, does that still happen with us, an anomalous leaning or desire for something extra, along with the blood of Jesus, that will ensure we have the complete freedom with him that we long for? The Hebrews clung to a dying, national glory, hoping for a Jewish church initiated by the Messiah. Are we clinging onto anything other than what Jesus has done for us?

The apostle Peter's journey illustrates this. God spoke to him in his vision on the roof, 'Do not call anything impure that God has made clean' (Acts 10:15), but later when Paul found Peter had reverted to eating only with the Jews, he was absolutely astonished that Peter could somehow be drawn back into something that so offended the freedom and joy of the gospel (Gal 2:11-14). That very system proposing a form of contact with God offered no hope for true and permanent access to him, yet the Jews kept looking back to this old Covenant life. One wonders then, do we still cling to practices and empty religious ways that hinder us from being radical believers? Could it be possible? Might Paul's words apply to us, 'O foolish Galatians! Who has bewitched you?' (Gal 3:1). Who has got hold of you and entranced you with something that is no longer valuable in any way? The Old Covenant is obsolete! Paul's cry was that, 'It is for freedom that Christ has set us free' (Gal 5:1).

The overall goal of the letter to the Hebrews is to establish the superiority and complete sufficiency of the work of Jesus Christ, which brings all men and women to a complete and confident access into the reality of God's presence. Therefore our prayer in approaching this book could be one of, 'Father, would you free us from things that we really don't need to consider or rely on, so that our boldness, our confidence, and our sense of absolute freedom in your presence is radically increased compared to where it is now?'

In simple outline, the letter to the Hebrews comprises a section relating to the person of Christ and the work of Christ, followed by a section about the application of that work to our lives. We are going to read about the person of Christ, trusting that the Holy Spirit will cause us to see him afresh, as who he is in himself. We are then going to read about the work of Christ, what he has done, the whole breadth of his extraordinary salvation; and then we will read about applying it to the great marathon run we all embarked on when we gave our lives to him. For this to have any relevance in our daily lives, we should be looking for ways in which we can appropriate what we learn for ourselves as we go through this book, so that by the end, our marathon run is more alive and aflame than it ever was before.

Through the letter, the writer inserts a succession of five warnings or exhortations. Weaved into the exposition of the person of Christ, the work of Christ and the application of the work of Christ, he places these really quite profound warnings, which are sometimes followed by encouragements. These become progressively stronger as we move through the letter. There are no warnings anywhere else in the New Testament quite like these in the book of Hebrews!

A number of recurring themes can be identified, threading their way through the book. We can look at these as guiderails to help as we go through. These include:

- the supremacy of Christ above all else (first mentioned in 1:2)
- the humanity of Christ (2:14)
- what Jesus did on the cross (9:26)
- the High Priesthood of Christ (2:17)
- the blessings and superiority of the New Covenant (7:19)
- the tension between the real heavenly realm and the passing earthly one (8:5)
- the tension of the 'now' and 'not yet', the present age and the age to come (2:8-9)
- our confidence in God's welcome and his promises (10:19)
- standing fast in our faith and being anchored (10:35)
- warnings against unbelief and falling away (2:1)
- the power of biblical hope: a confident and favourable expectation that God's goodness is coming (3:6)

There is a lot of material found in the other epistles that is not found in Hebrews. Paul's epistles or Peter's letters are often about issues in the church, about God's family, or about pastoral issues, which are not a major focus of Hebrews. There is very little about the Holy Spirit, and there is not much about the warmth of the Father's love in Hebrews. However, one of the things that affected my whole ability to understand this letter was to see it as actually being about sonship, about growing in maturity in our Christian lives by growing in our experience of living as sons and daughters of our heavenly Father.

I want to suggest right at the beginning, that if we can approach it through the lens of asking 'could this actually be about sonship and daughterhood?' it might help us to understand it more deeply, because it has made me realise that underlying everything, God primarily wants to bring many sons and daughters to glory (2:10). Thus the whole theme of Hebrews, the marathon of our lives, the running of the race, could perhaps best be understood by seeing it through this lens, that God's whole purpose, our loving Father's one desire brought about through the person and work of Christ, is to bring many sons and daughters to share ever more fully in the glory of Jesus, his eternal firstborn son.

A simple outline

Section A

1) The person of Christ [1:1 – 4:13]
  - Superior to the prophets [1:1 – 1:3]
  - Superior to the angels [1:4 – 1:14]
    - Warning / application [2:1 – 2:4]
    - Great encouragement [2:5 – 2:18]
  - Superior to Moses [3:1 – 3:6]
    - Warning / application [3:7 – 3:19]
  - Superior to Joshua [4:1 – 4:10]
    - Warning / application [4:11 – 13]

2) The work of Christ [4:14 – 10:18]
  - Particularly through his appointment as High Priest
  - He is divinely appointed – different to the Levitical priesthood [4:14 – 5:10]
    - Warning / application [5:11 – 6:12]
    - Great encouragement [6:13 – 6:20]
  - His priesthood is far superior [7:1 – 7:28]
  - It inaugurates the New Covenant [8:1 – 8:13]
  - Comparisons of the Old and New Priesthoods [9:1 – 10:18]

Section B

3) Application: the resulting call to follow Jesus faithfully, totally, and to the finishing line [10:19 – 12:29]
  - Confidence to draw near, full of faith [10:19 – 10:25]
    - Warning / application [10:26 – 10:34]
    - Great encouragement [10:35 – 10:39]

- Inspired by those who ran before us [11:1 – 11:40]
- Deepening sonship and its fruit [12:1 – 12:13]
  - Warning / application [12:14 – 12:17]
  - Great encouragement [12:18 – 12:29]

4) Concluding encouragements [13:1 – 13:25]

Hebrews 1

Jesus is superior to the prophets and the angels

In this first section the writer is considering the person of Christ, and his whole purpose is to elevate Jesus Christ in a way that he is quite clearly above the angels, above Moses, above Joshua, and above the High Priests, in order to declare his absolute superiority. We may believe that we know this as truth, as a fact, but let us allow the Holy Spirit to cause our hearts to see it in a fresh way.

Chapter 1:1-3

¹On many past occasions and in many different ways, God spoke to our fathers through the prophets. ²But in these last days He has spoken to us by His Son, whom He appointed heir of all things, and through whom He made the universe.

³The Son is the radiance of God's glory and the exact representation of His nature, upholding all things by His powerful word. After He had provided purification for sins, He sat down at the right hand of the Majesty on high.

1:1 The period starting with Abraham through to the end of the old covenant is approximately 1500 years. In that whole dispensation of the journey from Abraham through Moses and right through to Malachi, the writer is saying, the way God spoke was through his prophets. After this there were 400 years of silence. The way the prophets spoke, the ones closest to God through that 1500 years, was varied and intermittent: they appeared, they heard God, they delivered their message, and then they were gone. They came at different times, and they spoke in different ways. These were visitations of men who heard something from God and did what he said. They appeared to bring the word of the Lord from heaven at that moment, but they came irregularly, they had different messages, and sometimes their prophetic actions were quite unusual: for example Ezekiel had to lie on his side for 430 days (Ezek 4:4-8) and Ahijah ripped up his new cloak to signify that the kingdom was going to be divided (1 Kings 11:29-32).

Some of them carried a particular weight of message: in Amos we read of God's judgment; Hosea spoke of his tender love and his mercy; Isaiah wrote about his majesty, his greatness, as the one who has made the earth and the heavens. Although these were not unique messages, each prophet had an emphasis of some revelation which they brought to their time, and while they were each different there began to accumulate a consensus, a growing sound, that something different was coming. There was going to come an end to this era called the Old Covenant; this time was passing.

1:2 After 1500 years of intermittent prophetic words, and then 400 years silence, now in this era, God has spoken to us through his Son. God has appeared in a human body, and the word of the Lord is now embodied in a human being, Jesus, and now the Son is speaking. How different that is to the range of prophets, that suddenly the Son himself is on the earth, bringing the word of the Lord. Why were there 400 years of silence, with no prophetic word from God? Was it to cause such a desperation in men's hearts that when the Son came and he began to bring what he brought, people were ready? 'But when the time had fully come' (Gal 4:4), there was a ripeness and a readiness, where the Son emerged and began to speak, and human hearts were desperate to hear what the Son was now sent to bring.

God spoke through his prophets, and now is speaking to us through his Son. This is all God's initiative, not us trying blindly to find our way to God, which we humans do in all sorts of ways, but God finding his way to us and reaching out to us. It is he who is speaking, revealing himself to us; it is all from him, not anything that we can manage to achieve by ourselves. The problem with the yoke of religion without relationship, whichever religion it is or whatever it looks like, is that in making every effort we can to connect with God, we negate the power of the blood of Jesus shed on the cross, because now we try to add to the work of the blood, believing that this extra effort will achieve salvation for us. Therefore, the initiative of the Father looking for us and speaking to us is in fact the powerful part, rather than us trying to get it all together by our own strength. God has spoken and is continually speaking to us through his Son, calling us to respond in faith and put our trust in him.

There are seven things the writer says about Jesus, the Son who is now here, who arrived on earth when the time had fully come. The first is that Jesus Christ will inherit the whole universe: restored, redeemed, reconciled, completely made whole; he will receive the whole universe at the end of this age to rule over it as Lord. He will then hand it to the Father (1 Cor 15:24), and we don't know what happens after that, what that will look like. He is appointed heir of all things; no one else inherits the universe.

The second thing the writer says is: 'through whom He made the universe.' We know this, but it is good to remember it, that through Jesus Christ the whole universe was created: 'without Him nothing was made that has been made' (John 1:3); 'All things were created through Him and for Him' (Col 1:16). Somewhere along the way we are going to find out that he is our brother, our friend, but he is also this astonishing king of the universe, who gets it all at the end, and he made it all at the beginning; he is everything, he is all in all. Is there a planet in the whole universe where Jesus Christ is not present, where he is not somehow there? It is mind-blowing, and that is why we need to read the book of Isaiah to hear of the greatness of God as well as the book of Hosea to understand God's tender love. 'Through whom he made the universe' reminds us that we must not make Jesus too small, our 'buddy,' and we must not make him too distant in his greatness that we cannot connect with him. We are forever living with the tension of wanting to be as closely dwelling in him as we possibly can, to be abiding in him, but also recognising that we will see him receive the whole universe – yes, we will be there, to see the king get the whole universe and then hand it to the Father.

1:3 The third statement is that 'the Son is the radiance of God's glory.' Those of us who are sun lovers enjoy the times when we feel it shining on our backs, and we are invaded by a warmth which actually changes how we feel. So if there is no sun we don't get anything to radiate in us. This statement 'the Son is the radiance of God's glory' shows us that when we get close to him he imparts something of God's goodness and kindness and wonder. There is an impartation deep inside of us when we get close to Jesus, so that he continually radiates something; when his presence fills the room we are in, something inside us gets so warmed up because he radiates, shines, almost impregnates us with a share of the Father's glory; it gets deep into our heart of hearts.

Fourthly, Jesus is the exact representation of God the Father's nature. The Greek word used – *character* – denotes the impression or stamp seen on a coin or seal. That impression could never happen on earth; no prophet could have that. No prophet could be the exact representation of the Father's nature arriving on the earth, displaying what this heavenly Father is really like; it could only be Jesus. 'In these last days He has spoken to us by His Son.' It is really difficult if you cannot see the Father, isn't it? We hear about him and read the word about him, but we have to trust that the Father sent his Son to represent him exactly on earth, so that the more we looked at Jesus, the more we would say 'That is what my Father is like.'

This is a difficult thing to grasp, that this is what my Dad is like, an exact representation, like a mirror image of the Father in everything he does and says. When Philip said 'Lord, show us the Father, and that will be enough for us' (John 14:8), this is the deep cry of humanity: show us the Father, that is all we need, that will be enough for us. Jesus said to Philip, 'I have been with you all this time, and still you do not know Me? Anyone who has seen Me has seen the Father' (John 14:9). So Jesus is the exact representation of the Father's nature, he radiates his Father's greatness, he reveals the goodness of God to all who look at him.

The fifth statement about Jesus is that he upholds all things, he holds all things together by his powerful word. In these last days the Father has spoken to us by his Son. His word has an incredibly cohesive power to bring everything together; he sustains all things together. Jesus Christ is fully in charge of every star in the universe, billions of light years away, and holds it in its right place, while at the same time he looks after each one of us intimately and even knows every hair on our heads. This brings into view the wonder of his immanence and his transcendence, his immediacy and closeness to us, and his enormity as the king who rules the universe, holding everything together.

The power of Jesus' anointed word is fascinating – it seems to bring everything together in a way nothing else can. The things in us that are of God can become scattered or separated, but God's word always seems to bring them together. When we are under the authority of his word, allowing it to teach us and reach deep within us, everything inside us seems to become centred again. That is a strange and cohesive power. Other things can make us feel that we are completely centred and where we are meant to be, but the power of his word is that it gathers up every part of us, of a community, of a city, of a nation, of a world, and draws everything together cohesively, centring it as God would have it be. That is why we should never stop the preaching of his word – not just to be preachers, but because the word has a strange power to integrate what the Father wants to be integrated in our lives.

Sixthly, he made purification for sins. This is a big theme in the book of Hebrews, revealing Jesus as the purifier of the world. That is the power of his blood, which we will explore in more detail, and which is available to every human being from the moment he said 'It is finished' on the cross (John 19:30) to his final glorious return. In that span of time any man or woman can be completely purified by the blood of Jesus if they will just receive what Jesus did for them.

After he had made purification for sin, right up to his return, is the seventh statement about Jesus: 'he sat down at the right hand of the Majesty.' The implication is simply that when he sits down, he is finished: his work is done. The whole reason why he came, is that after he made purification for sin, he would sit down at the right hand of God. We can imagine the glorious moment where he ascends into heaven, having shed his blood, and the Father says 'My beloved, sit at my right hand, you have done everything I ever asked you to do, you did it all.' There is a magnificent sound of victory in heaven, because the blood of Christ was enough. 'Now sit on your throne until all your enemies are a footstool for your feet.' Sitting down is a sign of complete victory; the overcoming has happened. As Jesus said, 'To the one who is victorious, I will grant the right to sit with Me on My throne, just as I overcame and sat down with My Father on His throne' (Rev 3:21).

At the moment when Stephen was being stoned he saw Jesus standing up (Acts 7:55-56). As the rocks were hitting him, as the stones were completely crushing him physically, in his heart he looked into heaven and he saw Jesus standing up. It is extraordinary – it seems Stephen saw the king get off his throne and stand up as though he was calling out 'I love your heart given to me in this way.' And so as the stones destroyed him he prayed, 'I forgive them Lord, do not hold it against them.' Then the king sat down, as the eternal sign, not only that it has been done, the purification of all men and women's sins for evermore for whoever wants it and for whoever comes, but it was also a sign that Jesus has completely overcome the devil. Now it is only a matter of time until all his enemies are a footstool for his feet. What a Saviour!

We can dwell on these truths: Jesus is appointed heir of all things; everything was created through him; he came radiating the Father's glory on earth, the first human being ever as the Son. Now it is the Son's turn: in times past it was prophets who brought the word of the Lord, a word from heaven spoken on earth, but now finally the Son has come to represent fully the Father to every human being, to say 'Will you now come back home to me?' He came and radiated the Father's glory on earth, and every human being that Jesus ever walked amongst must have had a little bit of that radiating glory enter their hearts, proclaiming 'There is hope for you still, will you come home?'

He represents the Father – there is not a thing Jesus did on earth, not a word spoken, not an action taken, not a glance, not an attitude, that was ever contrary to the Father's heart for all humanity to hear: 'There is a Father who wants you to come home.' He upholds all things by his powerful word, and after he had made purification for sin he sat down. If we could just see beyond the curtain into heaven, we would see even now, the king sat on his throne. Could there be any fear in a believer's heart when the king has sat down next to the right hand of the majesty of God? Is there a moment of worry in heaven? No, there cannot be.

The supremacy of Jesus

There is real power in declaring the absolute supremacy of Jesus Christ. It doesn't take a prophet to tell us we are in a world where every other name that could ever be named, every other idol, title, leader or spiritual entity, is seeking to gain credence for themselves and elevate their name, so that the name of the King of all kings is somehow suppressed in a way that should never be allowed to happen. So whenever we are lifting up the name of Jesus Christ, something happens in the heavenly realms where spirits begin to tremble because we have dared to confess the absolute nature of Jesus Christ. And when we declare how great our God is, we also join with every nation across the earth in declaring his greatness. No other name, across the nations, gets the credence that the name of Jesus Christ gets, because he will be lifted up in these days, even if the war between the kingdom of darkness and the kingdom of light is getting stronger and stronger.

There is something about enveloping ourselves with the absolute supremacy of Jesus Christ that makes demons tremble. When we are half-hearted and think 'maybe that wretched idol has some credibility,' we diminish the very thing we are called to do, which is to say: 'Jesus you are truly king everywhere, in every nation,' until every knee eventually bows and acknowledges him: 'You are the king and we confess it,' whether they do this voluntarily, or reluctantly when the end comes. So the whole business of elevating Jesus is not a lighthearted matter. There are noises on the earth at the moment that are attempting to distract our attention away from him, and so we need to ask: 'Spirit of God, help us to be so absolutely entranced with the king and his throne that never in our day do we ever doubt his absolute supremacy, whatever is going on in the earth.'

Sometimes we may wonder how this is relevant, but there is every relevance in us declaring his supremacy, his everlasting nature, and his all-sufficiency, proclaiming that he has all we need. We are part of that huge and growing company of men and women who have chosen absolutely to bow our knee to the king, and unequivocally to dismiss any other name that seeks to have any equality with Jesus. If the Spirit of God falls upon us and we get a glimpse of the heavenly realm and the throne and the king sat there, and we absolutely glory in the fact that he has already overcome, we actually increase his kingdom on earth.

Demons do tremble when we say 'I love you Jesus, I think you are the best, and I'm not going to hold back, I'm going to let loose the deepest cry which I was born to make on the earth, and declare: You truly are the King of all kings.' Then we realise that this is what we are born for; we don't want to be restrained or inhibited. We want the passion to grow stronger, not weaker, and not think, for example, that we should be a little bit quieter now we are getting older – quite the contrary!

The stirring of the Spirit is calling us to say 'Come Lord Jesus, come in your glory, fill the earth till every knee must bow.' Don't be fooled by what the natural world appears to be telling us – it is not true! It is a sound the deceiver makes to encourage us to think as the world does, perhaps because we look at the news much more than we look at Jesus. What would be the point of being on the earth if we submitted ourselves to other names, when the ultimate name who called us, the King of love has said: 'Come with me and represent me well while you have breath on earth.' When we get troubled with a thousand issues the king is on his throne saying 'Will you set your eyes on me? Will you fix your gaze on me?' Why? Because everything else takes its rightful perspective when we see him as he really is.

Chapter 1:4-9

⁴So He became as far superior to the angels as the name He has inherited is excellent beyond theirs. ⁵For to which of the angels did God ever say:

"You are My Son;
  today I have become Your Father"?

Or again:

"I will be His Father,

and He will be My Son"?

⁶And again, when God brings His firstborn into the world, He says:

> *"Let all God's angels worship Him."*

⁷Now about the angels He says:

> *"He makes His angels winds,*
> *His servants flames of fire."*

⁸But about the Son He says:

> *"Your throne, O God, endures forever and ever,*
> *and justice is the sceptre of Your kingdom.*
> *⁹You have loved righteousness*
> *and hated wickedness;*
> *therefore God, Your God, has anointed You*
> *above Your companions with the oil of joy."*

1:4-5 Hebrews has been called a 'book of better things' – far better things. The Greek word for 'better' (*kreitton*) occurs thirteen times in Hebrews, twice as many as the whole of the rest of the New Testament. It calls its readers to look beyond what they have had up till now, and in particular to see how much greater is the life we have through the New Covenant than that given through the Law in the old era.

What can we understand about the angels and the king? If we say 'Lord, give me revelation about that one thing that fascinates me,' he always responds to that request. 'Show me something about Jesus,' we might say. How beautiful that after the 400 years of silence there is never this silence ever again, because the king has come and now the Son is speaking night and day to all who want to hear him, and he will continue speaking until he comes back in glory.

In verses 5-14 the writer uses seven Old Testament passages, five from the psalms, to prove that Jesus is greater than the angels. The Jews had a huge awe and reverence for angels, not just because they are worthy of reverence, but also because they believed them to be the mediators of the Old Covenant. For the Jews, angels were of great importance because angels mediated their distinctiveness as a

17

people to receive the Old Covenant, so that they could connect with God.

Quoting from Psalm 2:7, the first point the writer makes is this rhetorical question: to which of the angels did God ever say 'You are my son and I am your father'? Did God ever say that to an angel? No! So in other words, the magnificence of angelic hosts, which we do honour and welcome and love to have around us, fades in the realisation that never did God say to an angel 'You are my son.' Why didn't he? Because angels are not made in his image, they are disembodied spirits, and therefore they cannot be his sons and daughters. 'Or again' – the writer to Hebrews is talking to the Jewish people in their absolute reverence for angels – to which of the angels did God ever say 'I will be his Father, and he will be My Son' (2 Sam 7:14)? He did not say this to angels, only to Jesus.

Angels

There are about 300 references to angels in the bible. There are also references to cherubim (e.g. in Ezekiel), seraphim (e.g. in Isaiah), and 'living creatures' (e.g. in Revelation). Who are they? They are created beings, existing since before mankind was made, and they are spirits, without having a body. They have emotions: they can experience joy (Luke 15:10), and they have free moral choice. They are described here as flaming fiery messengers (the word angel means 'messenger'). They worship before the throne of God continually (Rev 5:11-12), and they come to serve God's people in their destiny on earth (Heb 1:14). They bring messages from God (Luke 1:26-38), they protect us from danger (Psa 91:11-12), they can provide for our physical needs (1 Kings 19:5-7), and they can rescue us out of difficult situations (Acts 5:19). They are powerful beings sent from heaven to declare and bring about the will of God to people on earth (Luke 24:4-7).

Angels sometimes operate in a crowd – a 'host' or multitude. When the 'great multitude of the heavenly host' appeared to the shepherds on the hillside at Jesus' birth (Luke 2:13) it wasn't a small number of angels. In Hebrews 12:22 we learn that they are numerous and that around the throne of God there are 'myriads of myriads and thousands of thousands' (Rev 5:11). Jesus could have called on 'more than twelve legions of angels' (Matt 26:53) to fight for him.

They are powerful creatures, but unlike God they are finite and remain limited to being in one place at a time (Dan 10:12-14). There is a hierarchy, with archangels such as Michael (Jude 9; 1 Thess 4:16). Gabriel is the only other angel named in the bible, and his role was to bring good news to men and women as a messenger (Luke 1:11-15, 19-20).

In our time there are angels sent to guard us, there are defender angels, and warrior angels. Some people claim to have seen angels, and what they usually see is magnificence. We are not called to worship angels, and we are not called to voluntarily initiate conversation with angels, but they do initiate interactions with us. Angels are magnificent: in most references in the bible human beings tremble when they suddenly see an angel. Angels are marvellous heavenly beings sent on earth to promote the kingdom of God to come more powerfully than ever.

1:6 Jesus has always been the Son, but this is the first time the Son has clothed himself with a human body, humanity, when he becomes fully man. Now there is a new dimension to his existing sonship: now the son of God has become a human being, and is the first of a whole new race called sons and daughters of God. He has always been Son, but now, if you like, he is the firstborn son. The Son is now in a human frame, Jesus is fully human as well as being fully God, and many are now going to follow in his wake to create a whole new species called sons and daughters of God. This was never the case for angels, who do not have bodies and are not sons and daughters of God; in fact, all the angels now worship him as the firstborn son, as the writer states quoting Deuteronomy 32:43 in the Septuagint (Greek) translation.

1:7 The Son sits, but angels worship, so there is no comparison between them. The Son is king, and the angels bow and serve him and obey his orders (Psa 104:4). What the writer of Hebrews is saying is: 'When you are declaring this supremacy of Jesus, you Jewish believers, do not even begin to think that angels have any comparison with the wonder of who the Son is!' Whatever place angels have in the universe, however high that may be, it is nothing compared to the utter supremacy of the Son.

1:8 There is an order in Hebrews 1 that is absolutely foundational to the way of the kingdom: first God declares Jesus to be his son, establishing his identity ('this is my son; the Son in these last days has come and spoken to us'), and then he is also named as king. There is his throne: 'Your throne, O God, endures forever and ever; and justice is the sceptre of Your kingdom' (Psa 45:6). The absolute certainty of heaven's order is always that we are given our identity first, before we ever pick up the mandate of what we have been tasked with doing. God claims him as his son, and then he is also declared to be the king whose throne lasts for ever, with a sceptre of justice and love of righteousness. This order applies to us too: we are called to reign as kings and queens, there is a mandate on us, which is probably beyond our understanding, but first of all we envelope ourselves with who we are, our identity as sons and daughters. Only then does God say 'now go and fulfill your mandate.'

Many of us have been on a journey where we realise that if we try to carry out the calling on our lives without settling the identity issue, it all goes horribly wrong, because we operate from a heart that is more orphaned than fathered. We live as orphan-hearted children if we do not know our real heavenly father, because we derive our true identity from him – however good our relationship with our earthly parents has been. If our hearts have not begun to be fathered by our heavenly father, we cannot know our real heavenly identity as his sons and daughters. God is establishing a principle for his kingdom that proclaims 'I want sons and daughters, because they are called to rule.' But if we get it the wrong way round, the ruling becomes twisted by the orphan nature of our hearts; our hearts as orphans cannot handle that level of authority without our orphan-ness invading it and messing it up, which then damages people rather than redeeming them.

Jesus will reign for ever and ever; his throne is everlasting, unstoppable. 'His dominion is an everlasting dominion that will not pass away, and His kingdom is one that will never be destroyed' (Dan 7:14). The writer to the Hebrews is looking back to the time of Daniel, and is seeing the throne and the ancient of days prophesied there, and hence the absolute certainty of Jesus' kingdom and reign.

1:9 What is the foundation of the throne of Jesus? He loves righteousness and he hates wickedness, and this is manifest in the throne-room of heaven where right now the king rules over the whole earth. Are we allowed to hate wickedness? Of course we are – in fact we are called to, as well as being called to love righteousness. This means the calling on us is a very high calling to reflect how heaven sees things, not how the earth sees things. God is going to increase that awareness of what he loves and what he hates in a world that is now so messed up regarding what is perceived as right and wrong.

In the days to come, we may see shifts in positions of power, other leaders being removed, nations shaking, and we may see explosive events. In all of this turmoil and uproar of nations, we are called to be so aware of the enthroned king who is bringing in his kingdom in a way that is absolutely unstoppable, that it will cause our hearts not to quake with fear whilst many other hearts are really trembling. We may be in a time of uncertainty and instability of world events, but we are anchored so deeply to the stability of the King of kings on his throne, who is irresistibly bringing his kingdom there until everything is wrapped up and every knee is bowed, that we are not afraid, whilst many others are now in terror.

Our nation appears lost, confused, disorientated. The mood at times seems angry, contentious, divisive. But rather than us determining what should happen, we should go to the throne and ask the king what he is doing. Because there is only One who is right and it is the One who loves righteousness. The king is doing something in our nation that we can only discover by going to him, not by reading the newspapers. We can pray: 'let your kingdom come in this nation; whatever you are doing in this hour, Lord, let it come and let me not be confused or afraid, but rather anchored to the certainty that there is an unstoppable kingdom coming.'

Chapter 1:10-14

¹⁰And:

> *"In the beginning, O Lord, You laid the foundations of the earth,*
> *and the heavens are the work of Your hands.*
> *¹¹They will perish, but You remain;*
> *they will all wear out like a garment.*
> *¹²You will roll them up like a robe;*
> *like a garment they will be changed;*
> *but You remain the same,*
> *and Your years will never end."*

¹³Yet to which of the angels did God ever say:

> *"Sit at My right hand*
> *until I make Your enemies a footstool for Your feet"?*

¹⁴Are not the angels ministering spirits sent to serve those who will inherit salvation?

1:10-12   The declarations of Christ's absolute supremacy are concluded with two further Old Testament quotations: in verses 10-12, Psalm 102:25-27 is interpreted as referring to Christ, who was instrumental in the beginnings of creation. Without Jesus nothing was made – we are told that in John 1:3. He, Jesus, is the creator; he crafted the universe. He is also the finisher of this present age, wrapping it all up so that the age to come can fully begin. In 2 Peter there is a striking passage: 'But the Day of the Lord will come like a thief. The heavens will disappear with a roar, the elements will be destroyed by fire, and the earth and its works will be laid bare' (2 Peter 3:10). What will this be like? How is everything renewed? What does the new creation look like? Whichever way we look at it, the only unchangeableness in this cosmic process is the absolute kingship of Jesus himself. He is the 'I am' forever. 'You remain the same' is a strong anchor for all of us in the light of such a cosmic change.

1:13   Here the writer quotes verse 1 of the profoundly prophetic Psalm 110, which is the most quoted or alluded to psalm in the New Testament, and is always interpreted there as referring to Jesus the

Messiah. The right-hand seat denotes the very highest authority, putting Jesus next to the Father, not at some lesser level. His enemies, which are made a footstool for his feet, are whoever or whatever opposes his glorious rule.

The footstool imagery implies complete subjection and the end of all their power. A prophetic archetype of this is found in Joshua chapter 10, following the great victory of the Israelites over the Amorites: the five Amorite kings are brought to Joshua, and he tells 'the army commanders who had accompanied him: "Come here and put your feet on the necks of these kings." So the commanders came forward and put their feet on their necks. "Do not be afraid or discouraged," Joshua said. "Be strong and courageous, for the Lord will do this to all the enemies you fight"' (Josh 10:24-25). The ultimate fulfillment of that picture is of course what happens to all Jesus' enemies in the final victory, which is absolutely assured for us. It is going to happen, and it is not that far away either, when all his enemies will be made a footstool for his feet. We have to believe this as we observe the whole earth being deeply shaken; we have to believe that at the end of it all, every one of his enemies will be utterly subjected to him.

1:14   In complete contrast to this, angels do not sit in the presence of God, they do not themselves rule, but are sent from the throne to serve those destined to rule with Christ. We need to recognise and receive every single angel sent to serve us in our daily lives. We should also consider what the implications of us being seated with Jesus are (Eph 2:6). Could it be that our true authority as kings and priests on the earth is being uncovered afresh in the very days we live in? Picture our being seated with Jesus, his enemies being made a footstool for *our* feet, and thousands and thousands of angels being dispatched to minister to us, as those who will inherit the fullness of salvation.

Prayer

Jesus, we acknowledge you to be the Lord: you made all things in the beginning, all creation belongs to you, you reign in righteousness over all. Every power will be subject to your victorious rule as the Son of the Most High God. As you speak to our hearts may we be absolutely captivated by your greatness, your supremacy over all, your Majesty. May we be willing to surrender before your sovereign authority, and to put aside every objection to your will in our lives, so that we can respond fully to your invitation to share in life with you and the Father. We ask this in your holy name. Amen.

Questions

How do you find it easiest to hear God speaking to you through his Son? Do you give yourself time to listen and to hear what he wants to say to you?

In the events going on in the world around you, where can you see God's love for righteousness and hatred for wickedness being revealed?

Hebrews 2

All things are subject to Jesus, our brother

In this first section of Hebrews, the writer is describing the person of Jesus – who he really is, and his supremacy over angels, Moses, and Joshua. However, every now and then in the letter he pauses for an admonition or warning, followed by the application of this to where we have reached in our journey. Often this warning and application are coupled with a strong encouragement, and the first of these will be looked at now. Why do we need admonition as pilgrims on a journey? Because we might be veering off the right track, or we might even be forgetting which way we are going. We occasionally talk about 'ad-monishing one another,' which means putting back into our minds what we may have lost.

Chapter 2:1-4

¹We must pay closer attention, therefore, to what we have heard, so that we do not drift away. ²For if the message spoken by angels was binding, and every transgression and disobedience received its just punishment, ³how shall we escape if we neglect such a great salvation?

This salvation was first announced by the Lord, was confirmed to us by those who heard Him, ⁴and was affirmed by God through signs, wonders, various miracles, and gifts of the Holy Spirit distributed according to His will.

2:1 Some of the warnings in Hebrews are really quite sobering, and so we must approach them in a balanced way: not being overwhelmed or over anxious about them, but neither dismissing them as if the writer was overstating his point. The warnings are there because we need them. The language isn't language we are used to using, but it is important that in the turbulence of our times we hear what we need to hear in them, without it robbing us of our peace, yet nevertheless having a degree of trembling inside us that alerts us to take heed. Here we see the writer warning us to 'pay closer attention,' by using the metaphor of a ship being well anchored deep down on the seabed, well moored by what we have heard, which is our anchor. If we are not anchored by what we have heard, we might 'drift' away, like a ship that has carelessly been allowed to slip past the harbour because the captain hadn't allowed for the winds and the waves that took it that way.

Drifting away isn't a once-only decision where suddenly, out of the blue, one might say 'That's it, I don't believe any more, I'm finished with this.' It is not like that. The drift away is really subtle. Perhaps in our journeys we have encountered others who have become unhooked from their faith, and our hearts have really been knocked back by this as it seemed to happen quite suddenly, in a single day's decision. In fact that one day was the consequence of a drift that began quite far back, but wasn't stopped, because the anchor wasn't in deep enough to moor them securely. The drift began to take them in a direction that wasn't obvious at first, but as it developed it drew them further away from the anchor point, until eventually the final outcome was for them to leave their faith, even after many years.

Sometimes we can see this happen in people who may have been really zealous and passionate for the Lord, but at one point they became wounded. Soon after this they began to embark on a questioning of their faith that seemed initially to be about rather peripheral issues. However, if they persisted, those questions started to be about much more fundamental things until eventually they reached to the very core of the faith, perhaps the cross of Jesus Christ, or questioning his absolute sonship. The wounding can cause questions to arise if the wound was never dealt with, and the drift begins with what seem like legitimate issues, but if they continue with questions rather than being anchored to certainties, the enemy can take them to the very heart of it all, and then, to everyone's surprise, they decide to leave the faith. The drift begins small, like the captain who is careless and misses the harbour because he didn't calculate for the waves and wind that would affect him, and then suddenly he is in much worse trouble. That is what the writer to the Hebrews is saying: pay even more careful attention. So in times of struggle or embattlement what do we do? We put our anchor in even deeper to God's word and the core beliefs of our faith.

The drifting can also begin when we start to lose our vision. A yachtsman can be in a calm sea when fog comes down, which becomes very disorientating. His sense of direction goes, and he ends up slowly drifting off in a different direction, whilst still believing he is going in the right direction. He has to look at the compass, and may be shocked to find he has almost gone 180 degrees off course, and only by using the compass can he get back on the right course. If we start to allow distractions or other priorities to blur our vision about the uniqueness of Jesus, or about his claims on us, the drift begins, and eventually it can take us right away from the core beliefs of our faith. There isn't another way to salvation.

2:2-3 Although it is not recorded in the Old Testament, New Testament writers understood the Old Covenant to have been brought by angels: Stephen challenges the Sanhedrin 'you who have received the law ordained by angels, yet have not kept it' (Acts 7:53), and Paul states that the law 'was administered through angels by a mediator' (Gal 3:19). There was nothing wrong with the Old Covenant, in which God spoke through the angels to Moses. It was a divine event, and so – the writer argues – if the Lord spoke then, and a violation of that covenant invited automatic punishment, how much more should we expect consequences if we ignore what God is speaking to us now?

The word neglect means to be careless of or have no concern for something; if we choose to neglect what is absolutely vital to us, and in making that choice we intentionally ignore God's word, we are bypassing our great salvation. The measure of revelation we have received is the measure of the responsibility we have. What the people of the Old Covenant were given invited pretty serious consequences; we have been given – as we shall see later – the glorious blood of Jesus Christ, shed completely for us. The greater the revelation, the greater our responsibility is to respond to it. This should not weigh us down, but it is true – they only had the law, whilst we have the person of Jesus Christ giving his all for us.

2:3-4 The Lord in these last days has spoken to us through his Son, he who has come as the firstborn son announcing this amazing good news. Angels were involved initially, but now it is announced by the Son and no longer by a prophet or an angel. God sent the Son to announce this great salvation, the ultimate answer for all human beings, yet even then two different witnesses have also confirmed it. The first witness is the voice of those who were with Jesus, who heard him speak for themselves. The second is the signs, wonders, various miracles and gifts of the Holy Spirit.

What do signs do? They point to something. When Jesus turned the water into wine, John tells us 'Jesus performed this, the first of His signs, at Cana in Galilee. He thus revealed His glory' (John 2:11). So Jesus' purpose was not for the disciples to stay with him thinking, 'we always get wine when you are around,' but rather it was a sign to say 'I want you to begin to see just how extraordinary I am as a person,' as his glory is his nature, now revealed to human beings. Jesus is thus revealing his glory through the sign of what he did at the wedding. Signs are helpful for us: they are pointers to something about him. We don't just marvel at the sign, we look where it is pointing to, which is Jesus – who he is in his glory.

The second element of this witness is wonders. A wonder is something that makes us catch our breath and say 'wow' – it makes us marvel at the spectacle. Perhaps wonders are meant to appeal to our imagination, to stimulate us to imagine things that God wants us to imagine, because they are the beginning of the fulfillment of something he wants to achieve through us. Thirdly, miracles are used – these are occasions when God chooses to intervene beyond the normal confines of nature, and we catch a glimpse of the all-mighty One who is constantly at work in his creation. They reveal the power of God; they are evidence of the breaking in to our world of the power of the divine creator of the universe.

Fourthly, the gifts of the Holy Spirit also confirm the great salvation. In 1 Corinthians 14 Paul talks about tongues as a sign for unbelievers, and prophecy revealing the secrets of a stranger's heart to everyone, so that he falls on his knees in worship and believes: 'God is truly among you!' (1 Cor 14:25). Paul also admonished the Galatians: 'O foolish Galatians! … Does God lavish His Spirit on you and work miracles among you because you practise the law, or because you hear and believe?' (Gal 3:1,5). So miracles and the gifts of the Holy Spirit were and still are evident in the church, and help to confirm the great salvation.

We need miracles, signs and wonders in the church today. Paul warns that when the 'lawless one' comes, the work of Satan will be displayed 'with every kind of power, sign, and false wonder' (2 Thess 2:9), which will deceive those who are perishing. Therefore we need true signs and wonders operating in the church so that when false prophets bring fakes, these may be seen for what they are. There should be no contest between the genuine and the counterfeit: the signs and wonders of the kingdom of God should outshine any others. False signs and wonders will not carry with them a revelation of Jesus, will not point to Jesus, and neither will they be accompanied by the presence of the Holy Spirit. Although there may be a certain level of the miraculous about them, they cannot compare with the genuine. We need more of the real thing, confirming the message of salvation we have heard.

Our task, then, is to pray in earnest for those who are drifting or have drifted away, that their faith may be strengthened. We have a responsibility for the part we play, which is to bring them back home again to an even more glorious homecoming than when they were first walking with God.

Chapter 2:5-9

5For it is not to angels that He has subjected the world to come, about which we are speaking. 6But somewhere it is testified in these words:

"What is man that You are mindful of him,
or the son of man that You care for him?
7You made him a little lower than the angels;
You crowned him with glory and honour
8and placed everything under his feet."

When God subjected all things to him, He left nothing outside of his control. Yet at present we do not see everything subject to him. ⁹But we see Jesus, who was made a little lower than the angels, now crowned with glory and honour because He suffered death, so that by the grace of God He might taste death for everyone.

2:5-6 The writer continues to elevate the person of Christ and his supremacy. Having established his superiority over angels he now continues by stating it is not to angels that Jesus has subjected the world to come but to mankind. So who is mankind, that this should be said of us? Who are we? We would not want to get to the end of our time on earth and realise there were whole dimensions about us that we never discovered, leaving us short-changed in this run we are on. Here we need to avoid a wrong triumphalism on the one hand, but neither do we want to end up with a negative, low view of mankind either. Both are pitfalls either side of the truth of who God says we really are in his view. My journey has come from more of a low 'wormlike' view of myself rather than some sort of prideful 'look at who I am,' but nevertheless there are too many signs in the scriptures that give a stunning indication of what God has really done for us and why his mind is so full of us. So while avoiding the pitfalls of too high or too low a view of ourselves, we do want to ask 'what do you say, Father, about why I am on the earth?'

This is so important to us because we need to understand in an ever-deeper way our identity as sons and daughters – our sonship – and the mandate we have been given. We want to burn with ever increasing passion until our last breath, and not put up with a mundane monotony when in fact it was something glorious that he called us to. Being caught in a repetitive 'sameness' is terrible in the great marathon, because we should be stumbling into wonderful discoveries and thoughts about ourselves as mankind that make us ask 'can that really be true?' The devil wants to stop us finding out who we really are, because he is the great 'shamer' of humanity. He wants to shame us so that we never dare dream in the way the bible invites us to do about who we were really made to be, and why God's mind is so full about us. Lord, what is mankind that your mind is so full of things about him?

'No eye has seen, no ear has heard, no heart has imagined, what God has prepared for those who love Him' (1 Cor 2:9). We might read this verse only to then go back to our mundane, boring everyday life. We must find a way of living with this tension between the height of who mankind is and the mundaneness of day-to-day life. The writer again quotes from the Old Testament scriptures to address this. Throughout the book he is constantly referring back to the Old Testament, not just to support each statement he makes, but because the Jews he was writing to needed to understand that their heritage was a prophetic pointer, not a home they were to stay in. Their scriptures point to what is yet to come.

2:7-9 This passage (Psa 8:4-6) is one of those places in scripture where the Septuagint (Greek) translation of the Old Testament used by the author differs from the Hebrew original: while the Septuagint reads either 'you made him a little lower than the angels' or 'you made him for a little while lower than the angels,' the Hebrew says 'you have made him a little lower than God (Elohim).' It appears that this seemed to the Septuagint translators too great a statement to be made about mankind, and so they interpreted it as 'lower than angels.'

What this appears to say is that the measure of glory and honour that God put upon his image-bearers, which is who we are, is so astonishing that if he went any further it would violate his supremacy as God. However, we live in a world where the enemy's tactic of shaming us constantly minimises who we are, never wanting us to fulfill our nature as image-bearers. After the Father bestowed the original glory on Adam and Eve, crowning them with glory and honour in a weighty affirmation of their nature as image-bearers, then the enemy came along and shamed human beings through sin, robbing them of that status.

But now the Lord Jesus, the Son has come, to restore our identity. He brings a tension into being: 'when God subjected all things to him, He left nothing outside of his control.' The 'him' is us – humanity. We were originally crowned with glory and honour, but then 'all have sinned and fall short of the glory of God' (Rom 3:23), so the Son came to the earth in human form, the firstborn, and through the shedding of his blood, he lifted us humans from the fallen-short state back up to the level of glory that was originally intended for us. And then he says 'I place everything under your feet.' Why? Because sonship leads to kingship. Sonship leads to rule. So the tension is: how many of us have yet seen everything under our feet? Has any of us reached that place where we see everything under our feet? No, 'at present we do not see everything subject to him.' However, more *is* going to be subject to us in the years ahead of our lives. If God's original intention is to lift us back to being crowned with glory and honour as sons and daughters, we can expect a fair amount to come under our feet as we grow in the discovery of who he has made us.

As yet we don't see it, but we do not have to pretend, perhaps by declaring that everything is already under our feet, Hallelujah, but then we go home and have a row because we cannot even control our own hearts. That kind of triumphalism would not be a sensible route to follow, but we could say that the more we receive who he made us to be, the more things *will* come under our feet. This is not just in our own lives, but we also see that world to come increasingly under his feet, as we declare that Jesus is the name above every other name. This tension between the 'now' and the 'not yet' is a process that we need to walk through. How many of us see more under our feet than we did when we first became followers of Jesus? Every one of us should, because we have grown in understanding of both who he is and who we are, and his call to us to reign with him is growing. Sonship always leads to mandate: knowing who we are allows us to begin to exercise that kind of reign.

'But we see Jesus... now crowned with glory and honour because He suffered death, so that by the grace of God He might taste death for everyone.' Jesus came as a human being, went through death for us, and now he has been elevated to the highest place of glory and honour. There is no question that for Jesus everything is under his feet, but it has not happened for us yet. We are called to follow after him in his journey and experience the same as he did, because he is the first one to go through it. Perhaps in our own lives, such rule and reign starts internally, a sovereignty over ourselves. If we haven't learned to rule ourselves, we have no qualification to help bring God's rule elsewhere. 'How much more will those who receive an abundance of grace and of the gift of righteousness reign in life'

(Rom 5:17). Only then can we start to consider ruling or dominion over other parts of creation.

Chapter 2:10-13

10In bringing many sons to glory, it was fitting for God, for whom and through whom all things exist, to make the author of their salvation perfect through suffering. 11For both the One who sanctifies and those who are sanctified are of the same family. So Jesus is not ashamed to call them brothers. 12He says:

> *"I will proclaim Your name to My brothers;*
> *I will sing Your praises in the assembly."*

13And again:

> *"I will put My trust in Him."*

And once again:

> *"Here am I, and the children God has given Me."*

2:10 This is one of the central verses in the book of Hebrews. 'In bringing many sons to glory' is, I suggest, God's prize in this letter. His crowning of glory and honour upon us is astonishing, particularly if we come from a shame-based background. We learn that glory is where we are heading for, and glory means we will be reinstated to his original intention, to the reason why he made us and why his mind is full of thoughts about us.

What does the writer mean by the 'author' of their salvation? Interestingly, this word in the Greek language (*archegos*) can also mean 'prince', so he is the prince of a whole new nation; it can also mean pioneer, pathfinder, or trail-blazer, blazing a trail for others to follow, or as if a ship that has gone onto the rocks sends someone out to swim to the shore and attach a line so that everyone else can now come across that line to safe ground. So too, Jesus goes ahead as a trailblazer of restoration to glory and honour as a human being. He is God but he is also fully man, and as fully man he went through death, he came out the other side, he moved into a place where everything came under his feet, and he says to us: 'I have blazed a trail, and now I am turning back because I want to bring many sons and daughters into that same place with me.'

Therefore, Jesus the great trailblazer had each one of us in his mind when he pioneered the route that no human being had ever gone before. While on earth, Jesus lived as a son and he fellowshipped with the Father; he went through death and he then came into that place of glory and honour where he is absolutely king over all, and he wants us to follow in this path, so that we too come into that place he is now in.

What does it mean that Jesus was made perfect through suffering? Was Jesus not perfect already? What did he need that he didn't already have? Yes, he was morally perfect, but he needed to experience a fuller identification with us: if he was blazing a trail that allows all of us to come back to glory, he had to go through the suffering of being on the earth where he was rejected, betrayed, and physically tortured with awful suffering, as well as experience the torment of temptation. He had to go through all this so that when he became a high priest he had already fully experienced humanity, to be able to represent us fully before the Father's throne. Perfect here means complete, not sinless.

In that light, perhaps we should have a better theology of suffering in the church, especially for the more 'charismatic' amongst believers. We need to have a better theology of suffering as the route to deepening sonship, because if we misunderstand our suffering, we have misunderstood the suffering Jesus underwent, and we have misunderstood the Father. We become disappointed and disillusioned and we disengage, having never understood the deep connection in the New Testament of suffering leading to glory. Many believers have taken offence too quickly over God not being there for them. 'Why did you allow that if you are a good Father?' they may ask, and the offence causes them to withdraw from the true marathon of becoming sons and daughters.

We have probably all been tempted to think 'that's enough, I can't do it any longer, that's just not fair God,' perhaps when an old wound in our heart begins to come to the surface and confirm a false, ungodly belief we have made an alliance with. But if this is the way he has set for us, then it is unstoppable. Of course Jesus went through unique suffering in Gethsemane, but he set a new path for us. He promises that if we follow him, we will be lifted to places of glory and honour that we were destined to inhabit, but we have to go along the trail he has blazed for us.

In the secular world, people might wish their boss would come down onto the shop floor and sit with them and hear about their struggles, and understand a bit of their suffering. The boss might have his eyes opened to the issues and have compassion and love for the individuals he has met, and his heart may be moved because he has experienced what he previously only knew was true through reports.

Yet it goes far deeper than this. We need a better theology of this suffering as the route to a deeper sonship. In Hebrews 5:8 we read that 'although He was a Son, He learned obedience from what He suffered.' So even Jesus wasn't perfect in his obedience until he had been obedient through temptation and suffering. Being made perfect therefore goes beyond moral perfection, it is rather a completion of Jesus, being made fit for the task to be a high priest. There is ultimately, however, mystery in this: we can never fully know what it meant for Jesus to suffer as a man on the earth.

2:11 It is Jesus who makes men holy, and we are the ones who are being made holy. Jesus and we are of the same family. Jesus is not ashamed to call us his brother or sister, which is amazing! He blazed a trail, and we agreed to follow him on the trail because it leads to the most glorious prize, which is our recovering who we were really intended to be. As yet it has not all happened fully, but it is increasingly being fulfilled because the cross is behind us. With the cross in the past, we are learning to receive what he destined for us, and what the writer tells us here is that as soon as we said 'yes,' instantly Jesus replied 'you are in the family.' He is the prince of a whole new nation, he is the commander who has gone ahead, he is the trailblazer who has stepped through this process, so that millions could come in after him, and as soon as we start following, he declares: 'you belong, you are one of us, you are my brother or sister.'

It is as though there is a new species or race that hasn't been seen before. This isn't a company of people that has ever been on the earth, because only the blood of Jesus, our trailblazer, could open up the door and ask millions to follow after him. They become a whole new family, which the Father has longed for since the beginning of creation. As soon as we lose this idea of family, even amongst believers, we have lost the whole plot. This is because the Father always wanted a family, not an eccentric collection of people who behaved a bit religiously. He wanted a family where the king can turn to us and say, 'I am not ashamed to call you my sister, my brother.' This causes us to stop and think, 'What? The King of love wants me and my messed up, sinful, shame-ridden life?' but he looks at us and declares that we are now members of his own immediate family.

Being a true brother, to use actual family terms, is difficult to comprehend, but if we can think of a new race, with a prince going ahead who calls us in to join him, if we can think of Jesus saying 'I really do call you brother and sister,' that introduces another aspect to the intimacy we are invited to have with him. We can imagine his blood circulating through our veins; eternal divine DNA flooding through our bodies, bringing us into a family that has never been seen before on earth. Only the blood of Jesus Christ could do that.

2:12 'I will proclaim Your name to My brothers; I will sing Your praises in the assembly.' This is the first of three Old Testament quotations, which back up the claim that Jesus and we are of the same family. This first comes from Psalm 22:22. The name he declares to his brothers is that of 'Father'. He states, 'Father, I've declared your name, I've revealed who you are to my followers, I've made your name known, Father' (see John 17:6, 26). Jesus, having led the way, turns back to all of the family, and declares: he is your Father. And he sings this in the assembly of believers. What great images these are of Jesus telling us about Father – his Father and our Father. Just as Jesus reveals our Father to us, so the Father wants to display his sons and daughters, as his family, to the world. He wants us to be awakened to who we are, in our identity as men and women from his heavenly family, and then reveal that identity to the world around us – a world which is tearing identity apart, with ever more confusing ideas about who we are as men and women, losing all sight of fathering and family and true identity.

2:13 The second quotation, 'I will put My trust in Him,' is from Isaiah 8:17. This is significant here, as Jesus was the first-born son and therefore he exhibited perfect sonship on earth through perfect trust in the Father. In his trailblazing on earth he models sonship, and the very heart of it is this declaration that he has put his trust 'in Him.'

The third quotation, 'Here am I, and the children God has given Me,' is from Isaiah 8:18 and follows on from the one above. It is exciting to think about what is really going on here; heaven on earth means the Father is enjoying relationship with his children again, the Son is ushering them in as brothers and sisters, and the Father, the Son and the Holy Spirit are thrilled to begin a new race that was always intended for Adam and Eve but was stolen away. It was robbed by Satan the shame-giver, and now the Lord is uncovering shame and saying, 'I'm going to crown you with glory and honour; although you may have fallen pretty badly, I'm going to lift you up and I'm going to crown you, so now come in and be family.'

When the church loses its sense of family, it becomes an oddity to the world. But when the church holds onto the joy of the king saying 'you are my brother, you are my sister,' we can look at each other and say 'truly you are my brother' because we are in this family, not just exhibiting a way of life that looks odd to outsiders. If we lose this sense of family, we are being robbed of something very precious that the world needs to see.

The story of Mephibosheth (2 Sam 9) is a prophetic pointer, centuries away from the realities that dawned eventually through Jesus, and there is great learning there for us. Mephibosheth is an example of a shame-based human being, who was disparaged because of his forebears and his physical handicap, along with his whole family. In fact, his very name Mephibosheth means 'out of the mouth of the shameful one,' or 'out of my mouth proceeds shame,' truly a man full of shame. One day David said, 'Is there anyone left from the house of Saul to whom I can show kindness?' (2 Sam 9:1). The person he showed kindness to was an enemy of his dynasty because it was Saul's dynasty, but there was something in David, made after God's heart, who said 'Who can I show kindness to in the house of Saul?' Mephibosheth's response to David's kindness was 'Who am I, a dead dog?' The moving part of the story isn't just the welcome David gives him; it is where Mephibosheth sat at the king's table like one of his sons (2 Sam 9:11). We need to imagine this beaten down, crippled man, being unexpectedly crowned in some way, by being invited to eat at the king's table for the rest of his days, the sign that he was being treated like a son.

Therefore, even in the Old Testament there are these pointers and moments where we can wonder whether the Holy Spirit is signalling what is going to happen. There is going to come a time when the trailblazer will invite every human being to come on this trail with him, telling them, 'if you choose to I will lift you up and crown you again, so that what got so shamed and crippled in your life, I'll give back to you, and you will reign in life.' This story also shows why David is called a man after God's own heart, not because he didn't sin, but because he caught something of God's heart, his compassion, his mercy and his goodness. What kind of person as king says 'How can I show kindness to someone in the house of Saul?' unless they have something of the Father's heart in them?

Chapter 2:14-18

14Now since the children have flesh and blood, He too shared in their humanity, so that by His death He might destroy him who holds the power of death, that is, the devil, 15and free those who all their lives were held in slavery by their fear of death.

16For surely it is not the angels He helps, but the descendants of Abraham. 17For this reason He had to be made like His brothers in every way, so that He might become a merciful and faithful high priest in service to God, in order to make atonement for the sins of the people. 18Because He Himself suffered when He was tempted, He is able to help those who are being tempted.

2:14-16 What is the fear of death about and what does it mean to be free from it? Too many believers cannot even bear to think about death; they don't know what to think and they are so afraid that if they think about it, it will summon up spectres of either oblivion, nothing, the end of who they are, or worse still, they ponder whether in the end they won't be 'in,' they'll be rejected. They may have a fear that 'there is probably something about me that I haven't realised is sinful, so I don't know if I'll be punished when I die.'

The very thing Jesus did when he went through death was to take away its sting. The sting of death is the possibility that we may head into oblivion, into some awful otherness than his presence. Jesus took that sting and fear of death on himself by paying the price, so that by his death, as the trailblazer, we could look ahead at death and see that it is a quick continuum straight into the Father's presence as a son or daughter, absolutely included in his family. Therefore, as we head for death, although we may have moments of doubt, wouldn't it be amazing if we were so free from the fear of death that every one of us just saw a glorious continuum into a homecoming, where we are utterly convinced that the blood of Jesus has done it all, and the sting has gone? The reason we can look to the trailblazer is that Jesus also faced that fear of separation when he was on the cross: 'My God, My God, why have you forsaken Me?' (Matt 27:46). He went through that agony of separation and faced that ultimate fear, which is why we can follow him and do not have to fear ultimate separation from our Father.

Dying is only a homecoming. We should be in a place where we are completely unloosed from the fear of death, because it is a sign to unbelievers when they see glorious homecomings: they see something different. We are allowed to mourn, for others and for ourselves, but we don't mourn like this world does because we know exactly what will happen to us. We never have to fear that we are going into some dark place of separation ourselves.

2:17 Here we are introduced to a really important concept: it is the first time the idea of Jesus as high priest is mentioned in Hebrews, and it becomes a growing theme. This service to God is the second major theme in Hebrews, the work of Jesus and his role as high priest. We will explore this in more detail in due course, but the point here is that a priest can only take on that role if he shares the nature of those he represents before God. Jesus is more than just another human being; he is our brother, and shares every aspect of our humanity, fully human in every way, including the fact that we have the same Father. Jesus said to Mary after the resurrection: 'Do not hold onto me, for I have not yet ascended to the Father. Go instead to my brothers and tell them, "I am ascending to My Father and your Father, to My God and your God"' (John 20:17). We are of the same family.

2:18 If Jesus was tempted in every way we are, was he tempted to lust? Was he tempted to greed? Was he tempted to pride? Was he tempted to vengeance? We could go on, but yes – indeed he was. So the way he suffered on earth was partly the outward things that happened against him, the rejection, the reactions of others, the betrayal, the horrors of his crucifixion, but it was also the internal things, the temptation in every area anyone of us has ever gone through. This must be the case, otherwise he would not be a fit high priest because he would not understand what *that* temptation is like for us.

Temptation

Temptation is not sin, but we may confuse it as being sin because we feel bad when we are being tempted. Sin comes in if we let temptation continue until it births something (James 1:14-15), but being tempted in itself isn't sin, it is just part of being in the world, where the devil acts as the Tempter.

To be a faithful and merciful high priest, Jesus had to encounter every temptation humanity has ever experienced, the whole range of it. In fact he was probably tempted more in every area than we have ever been. In other words, he went to the furthest extent of every temptation possible, in every domain. This is important because it tells us that there is no situation we have been in where he does not understand what that feels like, and therefore as a high priest he raises his hands in intercession on our behalf, preventing it from birthing into sin, leaving us victorious over it. If we ever feel bad when we are being tempted, then we can imagine the high priest at that very moment with his hands lifted on our behalf, so that we will win and not fall into sin. The alternative is that we think we are on our own, or that we are not doing well because most people around us are actually decent saints and wouldn't get tempted like this. We don't think that others get tempted the way we do, because when we experience temptation we feel soiled in some way and we assume it is our fault.

'No temptation has seized you except what is common to man' (1 Cor 10:13). 'Seized' implies there isn't a warning beforehand, as though: 'I'm going to come and tempt you in a minute, are you ready?' It seizes us when we are least expecting it, and each temptation is common to man, so we can be reassured: 'I'm not a hopeless case who cannot control myself.' The lie of the enemy is that you are the flawed one and no other believer gets into this mess. That is a horror, because we actually start to believe nobody is as bad as we are, but in fact all of his children get 'seized'. The devil as the tempter likes to make us feel alone in it and that we have failed, and thus give in to the sin because we think 'what's the point, if I go over the edge, I go down.' It is the isolation that the devil uses against us. However, in every temptation God provides a way of escape, he is faithful, and provides a way out.

He will not let us be tempted beyond what we can bear – that is not always how it feels, but that is what is true – and when we are tempted he provides a way out, so that we can stand up under it. The 'seizing' makes us feel we are going to go under, but God says 'I'm not going to let you go beyond what you can bear, but as you are in the middle of it I am going to support and strengthen you and give you grace, so that you actually stand up under the weight of it and come out the other side. I will give you a way of escape.' God will show us the way out, whatever that is. Sometimes it is just running away from it, sometimes it is turning the screen off, whatever it takes we will do it because grace has come; all he wants us to do is to stand up under the temptation. The high priest has been made ready to intercede on our behalf because he went to the full extent of every temptation that is possible for any man or woman ever to experience; he went to the end but he never sinned. That makes him a faithful and merciful high priest.

God never puts temptation in front of us to see how we will respond. We can blame the devil outright, but of course if we have allowed our own appetites to be unchecked by not ruling them, then we are more easily tempted by our own evil desire, and we need to take responsibility for this sinful pursuit of our own way. We may also find that times come in the marathon of life where there is a particularly intense period of temptation, which really tries to get a hold of us, and which may go on for days at a time. It is like a fierce battle, whatever it is about. It could be forgiveness, it could be lust, it could be anything. These are the times when the high priest lifts his hands the most for us, so that afterwards we will come out unscathed and stronger than ever in the assurance of who he made us. 'Because He Himself suffered when He was tempted, He is able to help those who are being tempted' (2:18).

Part of my experience of temptation is that sometimes it comes in waves in my life, and I mistake it for sin, which in turn leads me to pull away slightly from God, thinking he is displeased. At such moments, I don't have access to the very power he wants to give me to stop me going into sin, because I actually withdraw, thinking I've gone into sin despite only being tempted. This is a very important distinction. God is faithful and he will not let us be tempted beyond what we can bear. We need to ask the Lord to teach us how to stand up in the midst of the pressure of temptation and to understand it is not sin, it is just a moment that we can come out of; there is always a way of escape the Father wants to give us. We can have confidence in approaching the throne of grace in our times of need, and receive his mercy and grace in our temptation and weakness.

Prayer

Father, we thank you that you sent your Son Jesus to be the trailblazer for us, to find a way through death, back to life with you. We thank you that you have eternally loved us and chosen us to be your sons and daughters, to share in the life you have with Jesus and the Holy Spirit. We choose now to live as your children, with the dignity and honour of sons and daughters of the Most High. We ask you for the grace not to drift away when suffering or temptation meet us, but to remember who you have called us to be. We pray this in Jesus' name. Amen.

Questions

Has there been a time in the past when you have 'drifted' away from the message of salvation? If so, how and why do you think this may have started?

What is there in your experience of church life of God's people being a real family, being brought to glory as his sons and daughters? How does it feel that Jesus is not ashamed to call you his brother or sister?

Hebrews 3

Jesus is superior to Moses

In continuing through Hebrews 3, the writer maintains the emphasis on the person of Jesus Christ. We have had just a glimpse of who Jesus really is. Because is it addressed to Jews, the letter to the Hebrews focuses on certain venerated things to describe how supremely above them all Jesus Christ is: the prophets, the angels, and now Moses. For us contemporary readers, it may seem straightforward to acknowledge that Jesus is greater than Moses, but we may find some deeper learning which comes home to us as we read through the chapter.

We can imagine that this third comparison concerning Moses was a huge issue to the Jews. It can be alarming when we have been moving along one part of our journey in the faith, or even our narrative of life, and then the Lord says: 'that time is coming to an end now, you need to move into something new.' It is frightening how hard it is to completely shut something off that has been important to us, in order that we can embrace something that is new that the Lord now says is important. The story of Peter in Acts 10 exemplifies this: it was such a huge issue for Peter that the Lord had to speak to him on the roof three times, 'Peter, let me show you,' and he could not understand it. The Lord had put Peter into a trance, perhaps to detach him as best as possible from everything to do with his normal way of thinking; then he dropped down the sheets holding the unclean animals three times and said 'get up, Peter, kill and eat!' The massive paradigm shift Peter had to go through is evident because he replied 'No, Lord,' – which you could call a spiritual oxymoron. It was the Lord speaking to him, telling him what God wanted him to do, but Peter was saying, 'No you don't understand, remember the way we have come Lord, that cannot be so, that the gentiles are now going to come into the kingdom as well.'

This passage is startling because the radical change of thinking Peter underwent led to a harvest. Therefore if we want to see fruit we always have to be ready to leave behind things we thought were to be venerated. The Lord is saying 'they are no longer my ways for you, you will have to leave them behind; if you allow them to carry on, they will diminish the wonder of what I'm really wanting to do.' We need to consider this paradigm. We might think that we are not fixed on the teaching of Moses, but the prophetic application must be to ask ourselves whether God is calling us to something new. This would mean we have to stop doing something that we have been used to doing in our journey, whether it is a spiritual practice, or ways of living our lives, or anything else. There are moments when the Lord says to us: 'I'm closing that part, and you must move on – don't you see I'm doing a new thing?' (see Isa 43:18-19).

Chapter 3:1-6

¹Therefore, holy brothers, who share in the heavenly calling, set your focus on Jesus, the apostle and high priest whom we confess. ²He was faithful to the One who appointed Him, just as Moses was faithful in all God's house.

³For Jesus has been counted worthy of greater glory than Moses, just as the builder of a house has greater honour than the house itself. ⁴And every house is built by someone, but God is the builder of everything.

⁵Now Moses was faithful as a servant in all God's house, testifying to what would be spoken later. ⁶But Christ is faithful as the Son over God's house. And we are His house, if we hold firmly to our confidence and the hope of which we boast.

3:1 The writer encourages us as holy brothers and sisters, members of the same family who share in the same heavenly calling, to set our focus and our thoughts on Jesus, to give greater attention still to him. As we continue to work through this letter to the

Hebrews, may the Holy Spirit refocus us gradually, so that Jesus becomes so central to our lives that we only desire to do his will, and that we are completely in love with him. Let us ask him: 'Holy Spirit, please help us to stay on track with you, keep illuminating things for us so that we glimpse truth that adds to our journey. Lord, wherever we are clinging onto something, would you please help us to open up our hands and let go of what you don't want us to have in this part of our journey.'

Jesus is called both the apostle and high priest. An apostle is someone who is sent, and Jesus Christ was sent by the Father. He said: 'I have not come on My own accord, but He who sent Me is true. You do not know Him, but I know Him, because I am from Him and He sent Me' (John 7:28-29). Jesus was sent by the Father from heaven to the earth as the trailblazer, with good news for all men and women everywhere. He was sent, so he is an apostle. But here we read that he is also the high priest, so he has those two titles in this section; Jesus is many other things, but those two names are what we are dealing with here. He came with this good news, and then he became the high priest that enabled us to receive the benefit of that news.

3:2-5 Next the writer compares Moses to Jesus. He is telling his Jewish readers to stop holding on to Moses, even though Moses was remarkable, he led God's people out of Egypt, he went through the wilderness, he was a most astonishing leader, and the most humble man. When comparing Moses to Jesus, there are two similarities noted, and there is one huge difference between them. Both were appointed by God: God sent Moses, and God sent Jesus. They were also both faithful: Moses did everything according to the pattern shown to him on the mountain, he did as he was instructed, he obeyed, he was incredibly faithful; and of course Jesus did everything he saw his Father doing.

However, though they were both appointed and they were both faithful, there the similarity stops, because Moses is described as a servant in the house, while Jesus is the Son over the house. The house represents God's people; even in the Old Testament, God's people were his treasured possession. Moses was faithful in the house, but he did not have authority over the house; the Son however was faithful *over* the house. Why is this a big issue? There is a massive difference between a servant in the house, doing what he has been asked to do by the Lord, and Jesus as the Son who has authority over the house, the head of the house. He is the head of the church, his body (Col 1:18), and the builder of the house – 'I will build My church' (Matt 16:18); God has 'made Him head over everything for the church' (Eph 1:22). That means there is a huge difference between Moses' role and Jesus' role. That is the comparison the writer is making, not to diminish Moses, but to show that they are fundamentally different; only the Son can have that authority.

3:6 It is strange that we often revert to thinking we are here to build the house. We can almost hear people say it, as though we have no idea the Son is over the church and he wants to build it his way. We serve, we do our best, but there is a subtle shift if we then start thinking we build the church, when in fact he says 'I will build my church.' If we slip into doing a task he never asks us to do, that makes it more and more complicated because we won't know how to do it.

Some friends of ours living in a very difficult situation in a war-torn country heard the Lord say, 'you have had your turn about the way the church is, and it's my turn now.' God was saying that they had a good attempt, they had tried building the church every way possible, but now it is God's turn. They felt that awe of 'Oh my goodness, Jesus you are the builder of the house, you are over the house, you have a passion to build it as you would like it to be built.' So often men come along and think they can make a name for themselves if they build the church, but this is never our role.

'Unless the Lord builds the house, its builders labour in vain' (Psa 127:1). We are never called to be over the house as though we are the ones who are building it. Perhaps we even need to take care about names of churches or vision statements and such like, in case they ever get in the way of Jesus doing what he wants to do. The Lord is stepping in and asking us to stop trying to build what he said he would build; 'if you let me do it you will see a stunning bride emerge.' Holy Spirit, please show us if we are trying to build the church our way, when that is your role, your place.

There are a lot of 'ifs' in Hebrews. On the one hand, there are some promises God made that are so sovereign and unstoppable that he is not depending upon our partnership or cooperation with him, but he is going to fulfill them anyway. 'Of the increase of His government and peace there will be no end' (Isa 9:7). 'The earth will be filled with the knowledge of the glory of the Lord' (Hab 2:14): it *will* be. We can either cooperate with him and be a partner in that process, or we can choose not to, but he is going to do it his way anyway. These promises are not conditional upon our response. However, there are other things in which our willing cooperation to go with him all the way does affect how much we inherit what he has promised. This does not mean his love is conditional after all: it has nothing to do with that, as we are assured his loving commitment to us will never fail and nothing can separate us from his love. However, the longer we go on in the marathon, the more we can look back and regret the occasions when we did not go all the way with God, because we can see that our unwillingness has diminished what we could have inherited at that point.

So we are his house, *if* we hold firmly to our confidence and our hope. Confidence or courage is a big issue in the New Testament marathon, and it features again later in Hebrews. Courage or bravery or confidence enables us to take risks; not a foolhardy kind of risk ignoring the consequences, but rather one where we have heard him and we commit to go to the edge with him, because we want to partner with what he is doing, even though we don't know where that will lead us. The courage gives us the necessary strength to go beyond our comfort and into a zone that we were born for. Courage is thus a very important issue, as is hope. Those two commodities are what enable us to hold on when things get difficult – to put down the anchor again and hold fast.

Is there anything that has made us lose our confidence or courage? It is good to stop and consider this, because confidence is such a valuable gift which enables us to inherit all that he has promised. Perhaps we remember what it was like on another occasion when we were feeling very courageous. If we have not been able to hold onto our courage and hope, it might be time to acknowledge 'I lost it back there, I lost my courage to fulfill what he put me on the earth for, and I want to get it back.' Then we can pray for God to restore it, because courage is a real strengthener.

Chapter 3:7-14

⁷Therefore, as the Holy Spirit says:

"Today, if you hear His voice,
⁸do not harden your hearts,
as you did in the rebellion,
in the day of testing in the wilderness,
⁹where your fathers tested and tried Me,
and for forty years saw My works.
¹⁰Therefore I was angry with that generation,
and I said,
'Their hearts are always going astray,
and they have not known My ways.'
¹¹So I swore on oath in My anger,
'They shall never enter My rest.'"

¹²See to it, brothers, that none of you has a wicked heart of unbelief that turns away from the living God. ¹³But exhort one another daily, as long as it is called today, so that none of you may be hardened by sin's deceitfulness.

¹⁴We have come to share in Christ if we hold firmly to the end the assurance we had at first.

3:7-9   Having completed the comparison between Moses and Jesus, the writer pauses for a second warning. When God's people came out of Egypt, led by Moses, they arrived at Rephadim and found that there was no water, so they cried out to Moses: 'What are you doing, where is the water?' They grumbled against him, 'Why did you bring us out of Egypt to make us die of thirst?' (see Exod 17:1-7). The writer to Hebrews quotes Psalm 95:7-11, which is God's comment on this episode; it is a really sobering passage – 'For they have not known my ways.' If they had seen the Red Sea parting in that cataclysmic wonder of wonders, if they had been through the Red Sea, seen the hand of the mighty God championing their deliverance and walked through on dry ground, if they had looked behind and seen Pharaoh's chariots mired in the mud and then the sea closing over them while they themselves got to the other side, you would think that for the rest of their days their hearts would think: 'what a mighty God we have!' Wouldn't they? We could imagine that their attitude would never change from that point on in their journey, so that they would always be marvelling, 'if he could open the waters up like that, we believe he is going to take care of us in the smaller things.'

However, not that long afterwards there was a small problem, when they ran out of water. The Israelites quite quickly did two things: they quarrelled with Moses, questioning why he had led them out of Egypt into the desert, and they tested the Lord. It is quite sobering. Perhaps we have seen a huge miracle happen in somebody's life, and then later that person turns away because God did not show up when they wanted him to the next time. The Israelites quarrelled with Moses and then they tested the Lord, asking 'is the Lord really amongst us?' (see Exod 17:1-7). Is he? There's no water: is the Lord amongst us? So that place was named Meribah – they 'quarrelled' with Moses, and Massah – they 'tested' the Lord.

This example helps us to understand the condition of our own hearts in the journey, revealing where our hearts truly are settled, to see how we can go from a magnificent miracle and end up quarrelling and testing the Lord by wondering if the Lord is still with us. What is it that happens which can make us move away from a position that says 'We saw him do that, we've understood his ways, so now we're going to keep in his ways; we have a small issue about water, let's see what he wants to do now'? Something in them was unable to make this connection, and the result was that they hardened their hearts.

How do we get a hardened heart? It can follow on from emotional wounds, disappointments, suffering, lies, life's hurts, but whatever the origin the Psalm quotation says: 'Today, if you hear his voice, do not harden your hearts.' We know that 'in these last days He has spoken to us by His Son' (1:2): we are in the era when the Son is constantly talking to us, that is the beauty of the New Covenant era, so why do we get a hardened heart when we have heard his voice? We hear his voice, but we do not do what he says, we just move on, and at that very moment, because of the very way our hearts are created, something enters and begins to harden. Our hearts are made such that 'man does not live on bread alone, but on every word that comes from the mouth of the Lord' (Deut 8:3), and the sheep follow the Shepherd because they know his voice (John 10:4): we are made to know his voice and to need his voice, but rather than doing what the voice says, our response can be 'yes, all very well, but I've got my life to live...' We hear the voice but we turn away and move on.

One of the amazing things about Abraham is that when the Lord told him to 'sacrifice your son,' the very next morning he got up early, made preparations, and set off to obey (Gen 22:1-3). There is something in the immediacy of that action, the quick response, the obedience – he got up early – without which a subtle hardness can enter. We want to be responding quickly to the sound of God's voice as the Shepherd; if the Shepherd speaks and we move on with no response to it, that is when our hearts start to harden. This is the reason that the Israelites' hearts became hardened.

3:10-11 God states that despite everything the Israelites have experienced, they have not known his ways, they have not observed how he loves to work and lived accordingly, and the shocking bit is then the promise that 'They shall never enter My rest.' We will read more about this in chapter 4, but the 'rest' of God, in this context, is about living in the promised land. The whole promise was that there is a land for his people where they are going to have a home, where they will no longer need to wander, where his provision will be bountiful and fruitful, where they are going to be safe and protected, and it is a land absolutely 'flowing with milk and honey' (Exod 3:17). That is God's promise of where his people will find rest as his family and his people, but in the journey there from Egypt, they rebelled for forty years.

Later on, the Israelites are reminded of this time: remember how 'the Lord your God led you all the way in the wilderness, so that He might humble you and test you in order to know what was in your heart, whether or not you would keep His commandments. He humbled you, and in your hunger He gave you manna to eat, which neither you nor your fathers had known' (Deut 8:2-3). He didn't cause the hunger to test them, rather he was saying 'No, I've allowed the hunger because I want to display my sovereign provision to you in a whole new way, which neither you nor your fathers have known, to teach you that man does not live on bread alone but on every word that comes from the mouth of the Lord.'

Thus the purpose of the wilderness, after this magnificent deliverance from Egypt, was to bring them into a whole new relationship with their God. In Egypt they had been under Pharaoh's provision, they were used to being provided for by their slave master, but now they were delivered into a situation where there may not be water, there might not be food, they were living in a whole different reality. Yet here the Lord says: 'Now I have you on your own, for myself, and I'm going to cause needs to arise, not to make you hungry, thirsty and downtrodden, but because I want to reveal who I am to you in a whole fresh way, that Pharaoh never could be.'

The purpose of the wilderness was to teach them his ways, actually fathering his people. When lack came he moved in with a supernatural answer; they were no longer under a slave master doing what he wanted them to do, but now they were under a father who wanted to father them, to shepherd them, to teach and guide them, and the wilderness was the training ground for sonship in order to enter into the promised land. 'As a man disciplines his son, so the Lord your God disciplines you' (Deut 8:5). However, they hardened their hearts, they took offence, they battled with God, they rebelled, and they argued with Moses for forty years.

Although they had seen what he had done, the Israelites had not understood the nature of God that lay behind these deeds. God had revealed his name and therefore his nature to Moses: 'the Lord, the Lord God, is compassionate and gracious' (see Exod 34:5-7); Moses had encountered the presence of God in a unique way. The Israelites had not received that for themselves. The psalmist describes this in Psalm 103, 'He made known His ways to Moses, His deeds to the people of Israel. The Lord is compassionate and gracious, slow to anger, abounding in loving devotion' (Psa 103:7-8). When they saw his acts or deeds, the people didn't always know what nature was behind them, they didn't know he was gracious and merciful and compassionate, they just saw the Red Sea open up, the pillar of fire, the manna, and the water from the rock. Their hearts had not been changed into those who obeyed, who heard and followed, but rather had been hardened by not listening and by turning away.

In quoting Psalm 95:7-11 here, which refers back to earlier events, the writer to the Hebrews is combining a number of timeframes: there is the time of Moses, there is the era of David and the Psalmists, and then there is the time of the Hebrews to whom he was writing; now in addition there is our own era as contemporary readers. The message is the same for us as it was for them all. In the marathon journey of our lives with God there are times when a wilderness comes upon us, but these times are never a punishment, they are times of learning and growth, a new experience of his provision and his ways which we would not get when there was plenty.

3:12 This challenge may appear to be irrelevant to us, if we do not consider ourselves as having a sinful and unbelieving heart, or if we are not consciously turning away from God. But as we have seen it may just start as a drift where we begin to unhook ourselves from the anchor, and gradually things get a little bit harder. Perhaps somebody may say something uplifting in a meeting but inside we think 'I don't know about that, I've heard that before, don't raise my expectations.' It is an inner, unresponsive hardness of heart that very gradually comes upon us. We don't want our expectations wrongly raised, but we do want to be inspired and encouraged for the long journey. See to it that this challenge doesn't overcome us, even in a subtle small way.

3:13-14 What is the remedy? Encourage one another daily. Let us pray for those of us who are journeying through this letter and have lost confidence, courage or hope, that the Lord will put it back in their hearts, so that their journey may continue on in this way. There are certain church settings I've been in where the level of daily encouragement is so good, that as soon as you come in you feel you are being inspired, or somebody has a little word of encouragement for you. One word in a day when we are feeling a bit undermined can lift our confidence up again: it doesn't have to be a big thing, just somebody saying something small and up we go again to our normal level of confidence.

I love an atmosphere where there is a lot of encouraging one another daily – it could be small or it could be big, but this is the remedy to the unbelieving or the hardening heart, to encourage one another daily. It is a simple thing: we don't have to make it up, we just get a sense of what to say and we think it doesn't amount to much, and they may say 'Oh thanks,' but inside their heart has just increased in confidence.

This is a great gift; we New Testament saints can encourage one another daily. If we call somebody and they seem encouraged by that, we are also encouraged because the well of encouragement has been opened up. We encourage someone, and our own encouragement is likewise raised up. Thus the whole level of where God's people are experiencing life depends on this remedy of encouragement against the unbelieving heart. We just need to look around and consider how we can do this, then the body, the church, will be functioning well, and we can all hold firmly to the end the confidence we had at first.

Sin is deceitful. This hardening of our hearts is a drift, where perhaps we excuse something under a pretext so that the reality of its bad nature does not have its needful effect on us, and so we become deceived. For example, we might hear reasoning like 'those circumstances were exceptional;' 'scripture can be interpreted in different ways;' 'well it wasn't their fault;' 'we need to be grace-based around here;' 'it's not that big a deal.' In fact, we are being deceived about the real nature of sin, because sin is robbing us of our glory as a son or daughter of God. Whenever we somehow diminish sin, it is deceiving us that it is not that bad, and then we start to allow it a little bit of space in our lives because we have allowed it to have some effect on us. Then it grows, and while we remain deceived about the real nature of that sin, it starts to have some power over us without our being aware of it. There is a deceit about it when we excuse it, however we do that.

We can see that process with the re-interpretation of God's word: a deceit that starts to wrap itself around something which is now becoming acceptable, despite God saying it is sin. It is deceitful and it drifts. In a broader way the whole notion of what is right and what is truth is being challenged in our day. Is there something that is really true, or is it all up for debate? It would seem that the longer or louder one says something, the more it becomes 'true.' If people dare to challenge this and say 'it's wrong' they are pilloried as being bigoted, as being intolerant, phobic, old fashioned; 'how dare you think you know better than I do, who do you think you are?'

Anything is up for debate, because whoever has an opinion has just as much right about their opinion as your opinion; opinion has become truth. This destroys the clarity about God separating light from darkness, truth from untruth; it undermines it completely, robs it, and disempowers it.

Chapter 3:15-19

15As it has been said:

> *"Today, if you hear His voice,*
> *do not harden your hearts,*
> *as you did in the rebellion."*

16For who were the ones who heard and rebelled? Were they not all those Moses led out of Egypt? 17And with whom was God angry for forty years? Was it not with those who sinned, whose bodies fell in the wilderness? 18And to whom did He swear that they would never enter His rest? Was it not to those who disobeyed? 19So we see that it was because of their unbelief that they were unable to enter.

3:15-17 God in his anger dealt dramatically with some of the Israelites who sinned by rebellion against him: for example Korah, Dathan, Abiram and their families were swallowed up by the earth, and the 250 leaders who were offering incense were consumed by fire (Num 16:23-35); thousands more died of the plague soon afterwards (Num 16:47-49). However, it was in fact all those Moses led out of Egypt (except for Caleb and Joshua) whose bodies perished in the wilderness by the end of the forty years of wandering. This example of the Israelites in the desert does have real application for us today: 'God was not pleased with most of them, for they were struck down in the wilderness. These things took place as examples to keep us from craving evil things as they did' (1 Cor 10:5-6). These events 'were written down as warnings for us, on whom the fulfillment of the ages has come' (1 Cor 10:11).

In the New Covenant marathon of life, in this race we are in, the need is still there for our hearts to be kept open and tender to hearing his voice coming to us, whether in his written word, whether by his spirit, a prophetic word, through other people – in every circumstance, all the time. His word brings truth: the culture we are in is so undermining of all sense of right and wrong that some believers can only respond with 'it's all grace,' but Jesus came full of grace *and* truth (John 1:14). The order is important: grace first, then truth spoken out of grace. We must say, 'I'm sorry, but that's not to do with my opinion, the Son has spoken, it is really clear.' The media and culture around us can be intimidating and this corporate militant voice can undermine our courage. But here in Hebrews the challenge is to hold onto what we have heard: 'we have come to share in Christ *if* we hold firmly to the end the assurance we had at first.' '*If* you hear his voice, do not harden your hearts.' The responsibility is ours to be hearing his voice and keeping our hearts open to the truth being spoken.

3:18-19 The writer has in mind the time when the twelve men returned from exploring Canaan. They reported back to the whole community that the land did indeed flow with milk and honey, but the people were powerful and the cities fortified. Caleb and Joshua were for taking possession of the land, but the other explorers spread rumours and fear (Num 13:1-33). All the Israelites grumbled 'if only we had died in Egypt! We should choose a leader and go back to Egypt' (see Num 14:2-4). Moses then had to intercede with the Lord to stop him destroying them by a plague. The Lord swore that of those who had seen the miraculous signs in the desert but then disobeyed and tested him ten times, 'not one will ever see the land that I swore to give their fathers. None of those who have treated Me with contempt will see it' (Num 14:23). Only Caleb and Joshua were exempted.

Thirty-eight years later, only Caleb, Joshua, and the younger generation stepped into the promised land. God waited until all the rest had died; he would not let them in because of their unbelieving hearts. Have we ever experienced one of our children or someone close to us who for some reason completely stops trusting us, or withdraws their trust in some measure? It is very painful for a father, when his child stops trusting him in the way that they really should, assuming he is a good father. The father really wants to be the best for his child, and it is very difficult when the child isn't letting him. How much more, then, when God wants to school us into sonship, is he grieved when we cannot go there and we withhold our trust.

He cannot get us there; he cannot take us into that place without our trusting him. This is a challenging conclusion to the second of the writer's warnings.

Prayer

Father, we thank you for your word, and we choose to come under its authority. We pray for ourselves and for our fellow runners in the marathon that where our hearts have been intimidated or discouraged by something, you would restore a confidence that is brighter and stronger than when we began this journey. Pour out courage and hope, and show us how to encourage one another to be faithful in following your word, because we want to reach the end of the race and gain all that you have for us. We pray this in Jesus' name. Amen.

Questions

Is there anything in your journey with God that has made you lose confidence or courage? What did you do or can you do to have that confidence restored?

Can you see ways in which sin might have deceived you in the past? How can you avoid being deceived in that way again?

Hebrews 4

The promise of entering God's rest

We are coming to the end of the first major section of the letter, which concerns the person of Christ. Here the writer introduces the final comparison, showing that Jesus is far superior to Joshua, both of whom were sent to take God's people into inheritance: Jesus into the New Covenant, Joshua into the land of Canaan under the Old Covenant. In fact, they both share the same name in Hebrew and in Greek, so there is a closer identity between them in the mind of the writer; this parallel was a recognised theme of typology in the early church. Here the focus is on Joshua, but it is wider in scope than that, and throughout there is an ongoing warning against hardening our hearts through disobedience. In looking at this section about entering the rest of God, we do not want to lose the sense of God's absolute fathering of us, because he is so affectionate, caring and kind, but at the same time we want to understand something of the warnings needed to keep us centred on the race we are running. We do not want to miss out on entering his rest.

Chapter 4:1-11

¹Therefore, while the promise of entering His rest still stands, let us be careful that none of you be deemed to have fallen short of it. ²For we also received the good news just as they did; but the message they heard was of no value to them, since they did not share the faith of those who comprehended it.

³Now we who have believed enter that rest. As for the others, it is just as God has said:

*"So I swore on oath in My anger,
'They shall never enter My rest.'"*

And yet His works have been finished since the foundation of the world. ⁴For somewhere He has spoken about the seventh day in this manner: "And on the seventh day God rested from all His works." ⁵And again, as He says in the passage above: "They shall never enter My rest."

⁶Since, then, it remains for some to enter His rest, and since those who formerly heard the good news did not enter because of their disobedience, ⁷God again designated a certain day as "Today," when a long time later He spoke through David as was just stated: "Today, if you hear His voice, do not harden your hearts."

⁸For if Joshua had given them rest, God would not have spoken later about another day. ⁹There remains, then, a Sabbath rest for the people of God. ¹⁰For whoever enters God's rest also rests from his own work, just as God did from His. ¹¹Let us, therefore, make every effort to enter that rest, so that no one will fall by following the same pattern of disobedience.

4:1-2 If we do not want to fall short of entering the promise of rest, how do we combine what we hear with faith? Perhaps at least part of the journey of staying responsive is that when we hear God speak today, we take hold of it and say 'Yes, he is speaking to me, I believe it Lord, and I'm staying close to you and your word, I'm going to respond,' and as we do this actively it becomes fruitful. There is something important about mixing the word with faith, which is our willing response of 'Yes' to what we hear, which then starts to bear fruit in our lives. Hearing the word passively without our hearts choosing to respond risks falling short and missing out on the rest that we are promised.

4:3-8 There seem to be three sorts of 'rest' being considered here. First there is God's rest: he laboured for six days and then he ceased from all his labours and entered a Sabbath, a seventh day rest (Gen 2:2). God's labours were glorious, divine, amazingly creative, and everything about them was utterly and beautifully born from his heart. He then rested at the end of his labours and remains in that rest. Secondly there is the rest that Joshua led God's people into, signified by the promised land flowing with milk and honey, with houses, fruitfulness, their inheritance, and all that is described there, but only he and Caleb from the old generation entered in to the land.

Thirdly, David in Psalm 95 quoted here says that there is still a rest to be entered into, another 'rest' that is for us to enjoy. What Joshua accomplished clearly didn't fulfill God's promise of 'there is a rest,' because there is still a rest to come, there is another 'today' that has now come, which of course is the 'today' that comes through Jesus. This is the day we are now living in, the 'now' period, so the final rest that this is talking about is the rest that comes through the gospel, prophesied by David foretelling what Jesus would do. Here we can see the heart of God shining through history – it goes right across the centuries from where the rest was prophesied by David because Joshua didn't complete the fulfillment of God's promise. David prophesied it, then Jesus came fulfilling the prophecy, and now the door is thrown open for us to attain the ultimate rest; any rest before then has been but a shadow and a foretaste. There still remains then a Sabbath rest for the people of God, for us.

4:9-11 What exactly is that Sabbath rest then? Joshua didn't experience the completeness of that rest; David said there is still a rest to come, another Today to come. God is saying, 'There remains, then, a Sabbath rest for the people of God. For whoever enters God's rest also rests from his own work, just as God did from His.' This is a little bit complicated: we might think that if God rested from his labours, the rest we enter into through Jesus means we stop all our work. Are we talking about stopping all work? Or is our work somehow wrong, and God's work was good?

Our rest is that we cease from all the work that we have been doing outside of his enabling partnership with us, outside of his fathering us. We cease from our own works, because these are our own efforts, our own striving, our own hard work, which comes out of our own orphan-hearted state. We cease from works that lead to death, all of that comes to an end, and we enter a glorious partnership with the Father where he now is truly God to us, living fully under his word. This is a wholly different kind of rest because our hearts are no longer striving to work on our own. We are not resting from working, because we were created to enjoy our work; in being created for love we now have the joy of working, but work that takes place alongside our Father.

The labour of someone with the heart of an orphan is full of striving, performing, being all about 'me trying to make it on my own.' There is a self-sufficiency, even to the point of trying to win our salvation by striving harder and harder to reach up to God, in order that eventually we might connect with him. God now says, 'it has come to an end, I have invited you to a place of rest, where in living with me I will be a Father to you and you will be my son.' The trailblazer has gone ahead and made a way, so that when we come along that pathway, our heart is in a place of full connectedness to the one who wanted us. Now everything we do is born out of a peace inside, that he will always be a Father to us. Our occupation, our ministry, or whatever we are doing is born out of a place of rest that comes from his fathering.

This rest comes from a submission in our hearts; it means an end to self-effort, of trying to justify ourselves in God's eyes or in others' eyes, an end to the futility of trying to please others in all we do in order to gain acceptance or love, and an end to the misplaced self-confidence that we have what it takes to make it to the end without God's help. All of this is the behaviour of orphans, who do not know the love of their Father, who do not believe that he is always *for* them. The rest is that of sons and daughters who truly trust that their Father is with them and has everything under his control.

When Jesus said 'Come to Me, all you who are weary and burdened, and I will give you rest' (Matt 11:28), this is immediately preceded by a statement about the Son revealing the Father: 'no one knows the Father except the Son, and those to whom the Son chooses to reveal Him' (Matt 11:27). In this context Jesus tells us, 'now if you are weary,' implying if you have been trying to live without that fathering, 'come to me because it will have wearied you, and let me put *my* yoke upon you.' If he is the trailblazer, that yoke is the yoke of true sonship – 'I will show you, I will teach you what the Father is like, and what it is like to labour alongside your Father with the heart of a son.'

Moving on from the New Testament rest, the Christ-given rest where the Lord says 'no it hasn't happened yet, there's going to come another Today,' now we are in the Today, this present era, and the Lord is saying he wants to bring us out from any yokes of striving to earn our way to him, in any manner. He wants to give us his rest, by taking that yoke off, and putting the easy, light yoke of Jesus on our shoulders. Every now and then the old yoke, the old 'rest' comes back on again, at which point it is really good to shake it off and say 'I don't know how that got on me but I don't want it, how could I live with that when Christ gave his all for me to be free of it?'

As Paul wrote to the Galatians, 'It is for freedom that Christ has set us free. Stand firm, then, and do not be encumbered once more by a yoke of slavery' (Gal 5:1). We actually have to keep watching out for each other, and pointing out to one another when there is a bit of the old yoke that needs to be shaken off, because it is horrible to carry that around in the light of what Christ did for us. He won the real connection to the Father for us, and that is our true resting place.

The Jewish readers of the letter to the Hebrews had been carrying out all the sacrifices, the customs such as circumcision, the feasts, all the elements of the law, and some Jewish believers were still holding onto these, thinking 'I know what Jesus accomplished, but we still need to keep doing this sacrifice, and keep this feast, and fulfill the law.' For us, similar thinking can haunt us in our journey, even though we may not have the Jewish elements. We have to die to the haunting thought that we ought to be doing something to top up Christ's work a bit with what is necessary from our end, to get this glorious sense of the utter affection of the Father through Jesus as the place of rest. Particularly if people have come from a religious background, they sometimes find it genuinely hard to shake off every last shadow of it, to embrace the utter freedom, whereas if somebody has had no religious background and just encounters Jesus, they might more easily say 'I'll have all of that, that's amazing, it's all a free gift.'

This rest comes from knowing our identity as a son or daughter of God, and from that starting point we then do whatever the Father has asked us to do. If we are not in that place, we strive to pray more, to give more, serve more, earn something; if we have come into that rest these things just come naturally. The rest of God means there is nothing further we have to do to stand completely clean and clear before him for fellowship; it is all done. That place of rest means that everything we now do comes from a different centre than we had before, because we had been mixing it with striving, trying to obtain whatever we needed to get, in order to be close to him. Thankfully, it has all been done, the striving is gone and now we are in a place of rest. It has been said 'If I never do another thing, he still loves me and I'm at home with him,' but while this is true, actually the joy comes more from being able to do things with him now. Part of bearing the yoke of Jesus is that we learn how to partner with his enabling in a way we never did before.

Chapter 4:12-13

12For the word of God is living and active. Sharper than any double-edged sword, it pierces even to dividing soul and spirit, joints and marrow. It judges the thoughts and intentions of the heart. 13Nothing in all creation is hidden from God's sight; everything is uncovered and exposed before the eyes of Him to whom we must give account.

4:12-13 These verses follow on from the previous discussion about rest, to which they are linked by the little word 'for' – the writer explains how we can make every effort to enter the glorious rest of living ever more fully as sons and daughters of our loving Father. The way forward is, as before, to allow the word of God to do its work in us – God is speaking to us through his Son – not to harden our hearts through disobedience to the word, but to take this a step further by allowing it to penetrate deeply into the very thoughts and intentions of our hearts in order to identify any hidden areas of disobedience, resistance or self-will.

This sounds a little daunting, but I want to suggest that in life's marathon, in the pilgrimage that we embarked on, there is a process where the Lord speaks his dynamic word, which becomes like a two-edged sword, meaning that whichever way it goes, it cuts. As it cuts, it penetrates, reaching deep inside, and as it comes deep inside it separates out the most intimate, closest parts of us, 'the thoughts and intentions of the heart.' Although it penetrates and uncovers anything the Lord wants to uncover, this cutting, penetrating process is *always* redemptive. It may be painful, but it is redemptive. Reading this passage is a bit uncomfortable, but the word of God is living and active like a two-edged sword, and as it gets inside me it penetrates where nothing else has done, exposing something, but – let me say it really clearly – every time something is exposed, it is because that something is getting in the way of love.

The times when that has happened to me in my journey have been painful, yet also the times of greatest transformation. I wish I could say transformation came most when somebody loved me or hugged me, but the truth is that sometimes the sword reaching inside me has gone right to the core of some issues, and their exposure meant God could at last lovingly remove those things, because they were preventing my close intimacy with him. Sometimes my friends have done that to me, and it has been painful because it exposed something I wasn't willing to look at on my own, but I needed a friend to highlight this. At other times I have been reading God's word and the sword has entered deep inside my heart at that moment.

One of the greatest times of this was when a friend, full of the love of God, took the sword and applied it to my heart, in probably one of the most transforming moments in my journey. She carried the sword that reached deep into some areas inside me, and that separated my soul and my spirit in a way I had never experienced. At the time I was angry and I fought her, because it was very painful, but I knew it was a sword in the hand of perfect love. A sword is trustworthy when it is in the hand of perfect love; if we know perfect love is on the other end, we can more easily accept it because we agree this awful thing inside us does indeed need to be dealt with, in a redemptive way.

We know that without that process, it remains in the way of our intimacy with Father, and we so want more of that, more of him. The sword is the only thing that penetrates deep inside between our soul and our spirit, and the sword in the correct hand, in the hand of perfect love, is in fact kindness. My whole journey was transformed after that because the sword went into some areas I knew needed exposing, so that he could remove them from me. We do not like it, but we need it, and we need it carried out by people we trust. We are not going around wielding the sword and just cutting anybody we think needs changing: it can only be done by the hand of perfect love.

Judgment

We often associate judgment with punishment, but that isn't biblically true, at least until the end of time comes. The real meaning of judgment, throughout the scriptures, is always simply a 'separating'. The root of the Greek word for 'judges' in verse 12 – *kritikos* – means to separate, to pick out, or to distinguish. The first judgment is in Genesis 1:3 where the Lord said 'Let there be light,' and there was light. 'And seeing that the light was good, God separated the light from the darkness.' It was as though the darkness wasn't good, but the light was good, so God now wanted to separate the two to make it evident that the good was not affected by that which was not good. From there onwards, in everything the Lord is doing in judgment, he is always wanting to separate out what is not good in us so that only good can increase, ultimately because the bad or the not-so-good gets in the way of love.

Therefore we should not think of judgment as a court scene with a judge, leading to punishment because we are bad, but rather we should see it as a sanctifying, gracious work of God that separates what is not good from us, so that the good in us grows. Mediaeval theology, reinforced by literature and artwork in many forms, has radically distorted the biblical view of judgment by this association with punishment, and this has affected our way of thinking in a manner that we are perhaps unaware of. We can struggle, therefore, to free our minds from this cultural distortion in order to perceive the truth: judgment is always a gracious redemptive act of separation of good from evil, until the end of time when we will have to give our account before God.

God is not after us to punish us, but to get to our core in order to heal us. The heart of this is that truth is really important – it states that 'this is right' and 'this is wrong' in heaven's sight. There is, then, a tension in our journey between exploring the wonders of his love, and the truth that things in us need to change, in order to let us see even more of his heart for us and his desire that we enter even more completely into the rest he has promised. We need our hearts to receive correction with love, otherwise we will not respond rightly. If we hear it through shame or fear or with an orphan-heartedness, we are unlikely to respond and move on in God's purpose for our lives.

In the middle of that process, it is the love of the Father that shelters us while he does some necessary surgery to cut out what really stands in the way of an even better life with him. We need to understand what kind of heart is required to inherit his fullness, the 'better things'. If we start with a hardened, unbelieving or rebellious heart, then it is a beautiful thing when the sword pierces the core of us in exactly the right way and releases us from past things in our journey, so that we can begin to inherit what was impossible while that hardness was still there. The Father covers us with his love while he does the surgery needed to give us our hearts back, and then the healing oil of the Lord is poured on the place where he has done the surgery, restoring our hearts.

Too many people struggle alone with an area that remains undisclosed. This then becomes an obstacle for them to move into a greater place of rest and inheritance. Somehow they cannot let that area be exposed because there is too much shame attached to it. Sin's deceitfulness has led them to believe that this is too painful, too difficult, too great an issue for God to be able to deal with. But when the Lord comes along and says 'Will you let me?' and we say 'Yes,' because we recognise he is a kind messenger, this prevents that area of difficulty causing yet more harm to us and allows us to receive more of our inheritance as sons and daughters.

We all need friends who will speak to us in a way that genuinely rescues us from something that we couldn't otherwise identify. By them pointing out the issue, we can then – if we are honest – recognise it as true. This needs to come from the hand of love, from a true friend; after all, 'the wounds of a friend are faithful' (Prov

27:6). We may not like it, and it may be painful, but at least it is not an enemy coming along and tearing us down; the Lord does not do that. Similarly, we need to be friends in this way to those around us that we love, seeking always to separate out what is not good so that the good may flourish and grow in their journey. 'Everything is uncovered and exposed before the eyes of Him to whom we must give account.'

Chapter 4:14-16

14Therefore, since we have a great high priest who has passed through the heavens, Jesus the Son of God, let us hold firmly to what we profess. 15For we do not have a high priest who is unable to sympathise with our weaknesses, but we have one who was tempted in every way that we are, yet was without sin. 16Let us then approach the throne of grace with confidence, so that we may receive mercy and find grace to help us in our time of need.

We now move on from the section about the person of Christ, in which we focused on Christ's apostleship, his being sent, and our response to his being sent, into the next main part of Hebrews which concerns the work of Christ, which is going to take us through to chapter 10. In this substantial central section of the book of Hebrews, the major part of the whole disclosure of Christ's high priesthood is revealed in an extended way, showing how absolutely superior Christ's high priesthood is to the Aaronic one in the Old Testament. Just as the high priesthood is superior, likewise the accompanying promises are completely superior. This will be a constant theme throughout this section. The work of Jesus' high priesthood is something of a foreign language to us today and, we may think, difficult to understand. Even though it was all rooted in the Old Testament, however, it is most instructive to us if we are to understand how profoundly Jesus' ministry as a high priest works on our behalf now.

What is the purpose of having a priest? To put it simply, it is to minister God's word and his ways to his people, and usher hungry hearts into a relationship with him through the means of sacrifice. God is really 'other' in his complete purity and magnificence, and our sinful messed-up lives mean that we cannot have intimate fellowship with him, without a mediator to go between us and him. The priest in the Old Testament is the mediator that allows mankind to be connected to God and God to be connected to us; he is like a bridge builder who is putting back the bridge that got broken down because of our sin. Where we learn a lot about this in the Old Testament, in Exodus, Leviticus and in Numbers, we read numerous chapters about blood and sacrifices, and bulls, rams and goats, offerings and vows, and a basin of blood being thrown over everything. After about the fourth chapter of Leviticus we may start to wonder how this helps us in our day-to-day work! But it is there in the scriptures. If we want to understand Hebrews then we need to recognise the connection, the parallels between Hebrews and Leviticus, and understand the role of the priest as a bridge builder. Furthermore, central to understanding the role of the priest is to realise that the power to mediate this relationship with God is in the blood of the sacrifice that the priest offers, never in us trying to change our own behaviour: this is as gloriously true for us in the New Covenant as it was in the Old.

4:14 On the day of atonement, Aaron as high priest went into the holy of holies, on the one day in the year, an awesome day of fear and trembling when he would go through to that inner sanctuary of God's presence. Now too, the great high priest, Jesus Christ, passes through the heavens to the very centre of God's dwelling place, proving his sacrifice was totally sufficient, complete and permanent. 'God made Him who knew no sin to be sin on our behalf, so that in Him we might become the righteousness of God' (2 Cor 5:21). Because of this ultimate, final sacrifice, the book of Hebrews constantly encourages us to hold firmly and cling to our faith. This is such a familiar call in Hebrews, and in the days we are now in, where the intensity of the war of the kingdom of heaven against the kingdom of darkness is growing stronger, truly the invitation to us becomes more and more prophetic, that we hold fast to what we know deep inside is heaven's great call to us. Some at this time are being shaken by the sounds of the spirit of this world. I suggest that staying deeply rooted in his word is one of the ways we can stay anchored.

4:15 This is such an encouragement to us. Jesus' very supremacy never limits his tender sympathy for our frailties. The writer here uses a double negative to emphasise the fully human aspect of Christ's nature: we don't have a high priest who is unable. The double negative highlights that we do in fact have the very best high priest who is absolutely able to sympathise with every aspect of being fully human, because while Jesus remained fully God, he was also fully human, and in that humanity his experience of being fully human gave him the necessary understanding and sympathy to help us in our weakness. Jesus is able and willing to step in to help when we are weak, as he understands what it is like to be tempted; in fact Satan attacked him with more than we could ever bear. Jesus has already been tempted in what we are attacked with, yet he never gave in, and so he genuinely stands with us on every occasion and in every aspect of temptation, and he wants us to win.

4:16 The key to winning is not mustering up our best efforts – that is just religious behaviour. Rather it is to come to his throne with confidence and receive his willingness to help us, especially when we feel weak or stained because of temptation. Remember that temptation is not sin; it happens to us all, and we sometimes confuse it with sin. Whether it is lust, greed, jealousy, not telling the complete truth, or indulging in a bit of gossip, whatever it is that we are tempted or pulled towards, it isn't necessarily sin unless we give way to it. The throne is there for us to find mercy. We don't get the punishment we deserve, and grace comes in a time of need, which is his enabling power that fills us when we feel at our weakest. God is 'an ever-present help in times of trouble' (Psa 46:1).

Prayer

Father, we thank you that you long for us to live more and more as your beloved sons and daughters, resting in your ability, strength and wisdom rather than having to manage on our own. We thank you that your desire for intimacy with us is even greater than our longing to be close to you. We choose to open our hearts to the discriminating work of your word, to separate out any areas where our hearts have become hardened, so that we can walk with you ever more closely in obedience. We want to know more of the freedom you have won for us in Jesus. Amen.

Questions

What does unbelief look like for you? Are there any areas in your life where you do not fully believe or trust God, or remain to some degree in disobedience to him?

Do you think of God's judgment on you as somehow involving punishment? If so, why is this?

Hebrews 5

Jesus is divinely appointed as high priest

Chapter 5:1-4

¹Every high priest is appointed from among men to represent them in matters relating to God, to offer gifts and sacrifices for sins. ²He is able to deal gently with those who are ignorant and misguided, since he himself is beset by weakness. ³That is why he is obliged to offer sacrifices for his own sins, as well as for the sins of the people.

⁴No one takes this honour upon himself; he must be called by God, just as Aaron was.

5:1-3 There are three criteria which any priest must satisfy in order to represent men before God in this way. The first is that he must identify with the people he represents; he is chosen from among men and is one of them. Secondly, he is aware of his own frailty, weakness, and vulnerability to sin, and he can therefore relate to the people gently, with compassion. He has to offer sacrifices for his own sin as well as those others he represents.

5:4 The third qualification for the Aaronic priesthood is that the priests could not appoint themselves, they were always appointed by God. The whole process was awesome: the detailed description of the appointment of Aaron, and him being clothed in his robes (Exodus 28 onwards), makes us aware that God was signifying an importance concerning the role of the high priest in a shadow form, with all the vestments, the tabernacle, the offerings, and all the associated vessels. The appointed high priest was thus bridging the gap between sinful man and a holy God, and this was such an awesome activity that anybody who did not follow that process fully was in danger.

Soon after their ordination as priests, Aaron's sons Nadab and Abihu offered a strange or unauthorised fire, contrary to the Lord's command. God has his ways, and we must live in obedience to them. It was as if God said, 'I cannot allow that behaviour in such a holy and sacred person as a priest, whom I've called to bridge the gap between me and human beings so that we can fellowship again.' So, fire came out from the presence of the Lord and consumed them (Lev 10:1-3). Such startling moments could make us think that maybe God is temperamental after all. But no, he just wants us to understand the awesome holiness of our being reconnected with him through the priesthood.

Priests were to be appointed by God. After Solomon's death, the northern kingdom was separated from Judah, as prophesied by Ahijah when he tore his robe (1 Kings 11:30-32). Jeroboam went up to the northern part of Israel, and decided he didn't want people to go back to Jerusalem in the south to offer the sacrifices there, in case their hearts were drawn there. He therefore made two golden calves, and appointed priests there who weren't even Levites, although God had specified that priests had to come from the line of Aaron. (1 Kings 12:25-33). It was absolutely shocking that a king would make the worship of God into something about himself and his own purposes, by setting up shrines, festivals and altars in the north where everybody would be sacrificing to the golden calves. He was asking his people if they wanted to be a priest and serve at his altar. It was appalling that some of the kings took such an awesome order of God and then turned it around in this way for their own ends.

Most shocking is the example of king Uzziah, who was a godly king as long as the high priest was in place – which is a recurring pattern that is seen through the story of the kings. Uzziah had a magnificent first half of his life, living according to God's commands. However, his heart grew more and more proud, and in the end he went into the temple to burn the incense himself; he wanted to be high priest as well as king. God had separated these two offices as a vital safeguard for how he wanted his kingdom to be in the Old Testament. The high priest with his fellow priests entered the temple and began to plead with Uzziah, as if to say 'Don't do this, you don't know what you are playing with.' As they appealed to him, Uzziah became angry with them – pride does that – and as he was raging at the priests as though to say 'How dare you challenge me,' leprosy started to break out everywhere on his skin. The priests were in awe and hurried to get him out of the temple; he never recovered from the leprosy (2 Chron 26:16-23).

Why are those stories included in the scriptures? They are not there to make us fear God as though he is temperamental or unpredictable, but they are simply there to make us be in awe of something so sacred in the priesthood, and learn that if we play around with it and contaminate it, then there will be trouble. This is an astonishing thing in the heart of love of the Father, that says, 'I so want to make a bridge back to you, that you can have fellowship with me and come home. Do not mess around with the way I want it done.'

In this passage in Hebrews 5 we see that priests were appointed by God: no man could make the claim 'I want to be a priest,' and they were required to come from the order or family line of Aaron. We will see the significance of that later. However, by the time Jesus came on the earth, the priesthood had degenerated so much that the high priesthood family in Jesus' day had been appointed there by paying money for it. It was shocking how it had degenerated from the time of Aaron, through Nadab, through the kings, through king Uzziah, to the point where in Jesus' day they had paid money to be the high priest for the sheer status or power of the position. Empty religion without relationship is horrible, distorting and getting in the way of God's purpose. God started something holy and beautiful, then humanity desired to take it over and have power through it. It degenerated into something completely human, becoming all about religious behaviour, with the result that it failed to allow men and women to have true fellowship with God.

Chapter 5:5-10

5So also Christ did not take upon Himself the glory of becoming a high priest, but He was called by the One who said to Him:

> *"You are My Son;*
> *today I have become Your Father."*

⁶*And in another passage God says:*

> *"You are a priest forever*
> *in the order of Melchizedek."*

⁷*During the days of Jesus' earthly life, He offered up prayers and petitions with loud cries and tears to the One who could save Him from death, and He was heard because of His reverence.* ⁸*Although He was a Son, He learned obedience from what He suffered.* ⁹*And having been made perfect, He became the source of eternal salvation to all who obey Him* ¹⁰*and was designated by God as high priest in the order of Melchizedek.*

5:5-6 As with any other high priest, Jesus satisfies these criteria for representing mankind before God in this role. First, he was appointed by God: Christ did not take upon himself the glory of becoming a high priest, but God said to him, 'You are My Son; today I have become Your Father' (Psa 2:7), and then, 'You are a priest forever' – that is significant – 'in the order of Melchizedek' (Psa 110:4). Here again we see the order where sonship precedes mandate, identity comes before the calling; God puts that in here as a reminder for us. The whole basis of this relationship is that the Father and the Son are working together in a beautiful way, which is to speak to humanity for the rest of their days. Why is that so significant? Because in a moment of time, the whole Aaronic order is completely set aside and a whole new order comes into being.

Here is the first pointer: God the Father is saying to his Son, 'you are my Son, and I am appointing you to be a high priest, but it is in a completely new order, the order of someone called Melchizedek.' As we will see shortly, that denotes something completely different from the order of Aaron. So there is an indication that a huge change is coming from what was present in the whole of the Old Testament, which degenerated into such empty religious behaviour: now the King of kings has come on the earth and the Father said to him, 'would you be both the firstborn son, and also the high priest?' This is one of the qualifications of Jesus that makes his high priesthood unique, and we are going to see more.

5:7-10 The other criteria for being a high priest, of identifying with the people he served by being one of them, and of having compassion for them, are also satisfied by Jesus. Becoming fully man, he was and is truly one of us. Having compassion – meaning 'suffering with' – also marks out Jesus' uniqueness as a high priest, different to the order of Aaron. Through sharing in our humanity, Jesus experienced suffering, and he learned obedience through that suffering, by absolute submission of his will to his Father. Suffering has nothing to do with the Aaronic order: other high priests did not identify with the people this way by learning obedience through suffering. Jesus' submission of his will involved prayers, petitions, loud cries and tears. If we ever have thought of Jesus as a detached, emotionless man without any need for feelings, we have completely misunderstood the King of love in his human form. His emotions and feelings were as strong as any human being's ever were, as the firstborn son living on earth. This is not to say that he was an emotional person, but he had the full range of all the emotions and feelings that any human being has had.

When was the greatest moment of his crying? Was it when he left the Mount of Olives and he wept over Jerusalem (Luke 19:41)? His whole being was in pain, with his deep longing to shepherd and gather Jerusalem, but they would not have him. Or perhaps it was when he wept over Lazarus (John 12:35)? He wept, not because he didn't believe God was going to bring him back to life, but perhaps due to the unbelief he saw, or simply the compassion and grief he felt for those around him. This high priest does weep alongside our weeping. If we think 'this is probably my fault, he's probably busy so I doubt he's that moved,' we completely misunderstand his deep and passionate heart for our well-being.

The ultimate depth of weeping was in the garden of Gethsemane. The Greek word in Hebrews 5:7 is *krauge* – a loud cry, wrung from a deep place of searing pain, which cannot be stopped because the depth of pain squeezes out this great cry. It is important to revisit this because in the garden of Gethsemane, which is the place of greatest anguish any human being has ever endured, which no one else has suffered, the Son calls out, 'Abba, Father' (Mark 14:36). This is the Son, most deeply at home while in the greatest place of suffering, saying 'Abba, if it is possible, take this cup from me, the

77

suffering of the cross.' This is the cataclysmic centre of the whole of God's story on earth now focused in place, one moment, and the King of love is about to go to the cross when he says 'Abba, most affectionate father, please if it is possible will you take this cup from me?' And then this is the key part: 'nevertheless, not my will but yours be done,' he concludes; 'not what I will, but what You will' (Mark 14:36).

That is the reverent submission which brought Jesus to perfection and which, I want to suggest to you, is also the ultimate forging of our true sonship or true daughterhood. This may be a familiar theme we are looking at, but we need to understand that even though we never have to go through what Jesus went through, which befits him to be high priest, the suffering in our own journeys which brings forth a level of reverential submission is actually one of the crucial places where our own hearts are formed in true sonship and daughterhood. We do not like it, but in our individual journeys, some of the moments of worst suffering will have produced a deep cry, almost like that of Jesus, and in the submission we learn in a profound way what it means to have God as our Father and what it is to be true sons and daughters of the Father. If we are in a marathon, we must have a right understanding of suffering, not because he is a father who wants to punish us or teach us some lessons, but because we are brought to a reverential submission to our Abba, our Father 'with whom there is no change or shifting shadow' (James 1:17).

In the end, it is about Jesus' willingness to travel that route that qualifies him for a different order of high priesthood than the Aaronic order. He was made perfect – not moral perfection, but complete through what he suffered – to be a high priest who can sympathise with our weakness. Going through that suffering completed his qualification to be our high priest. 'He became the source of eternal salvation to all who obey Him and was designated by God as high priest in the order of Melchizedek.'

Suffering

How can suffering lead us into a closer relationship with God as our Father? It might depend on what sort of suffering we are referring to. If our suffering came about because we wilfully sinned and continued in this sin despite his warning, that may not be the suffering that best forges sonship. He will still work in that situation, because he works in everything for good, but it is more the suffering from a huge loss, a terrible relationship break-up, or some deep disappointment when we so trusted that God would act when he promised to, but he didn't; these experiences produce something in us that is wrung out from the pain inside. If we then call out, 'Abba,' he is delighted that this is the response of our hearts in the worst of pain, that we would still somehow reverentially submit to him and go along with him, even though everything screams out 'I can't do this, I want to get out, you aren't being fair after all; you told me to trust you but you failed me, in fact it seems to have got worse.'

Many of us have had something like this happen that has struck the inner part of us very deeply. This is so important because unless we have an understanding of suffering, we don't always run the marathon well all the way to the end, because deep inside us there is a growing whisper that is saying 'I don't think I want to do this, it's not fair.' Now this in no way discounts God doing impossible miracles to lift us out of the difficult situation, and we should want to pursue these all the more, but we have to understand how the process works in the long journey to the finish if he doesn't do so, so that we can navigate the suffering with the heart of Jesus the firstborn son.

Some of my heroes are not people at the centre of things, or who are well known. They are people I watch on their journey and I wonder 'how do they do that? How do they go through that valley and come out the other side so radiant and somehow even more full of God, when they have lost all that they did?' Those people are my heroes. For Jesus, though he had the sin of the world put upon him, and the blood dripped from his forehead in sweat, 'Abba' was wrung out of the depths of him and the submission was incredible. 'He was heard because of His reverence' (5:7), his reverent submission. God did not stop him going to the cross, but he did hear him. What does that mean? Perhaps that is the ultimate expression of sonship, where God says, 'thank you for bearing with that horrendous cup. I add sonship and daughterhood to you, because of where you journeyed to.' Knowing that a father hears you and is there with you, is often what we most want to know, otherwise the aloneness in the suffering is unbearable.

One other aspect that uniquely qualifies Jesus to be our high priest, apart from his journey of suffering, is that he lives forever. Now anyone who is joined to him as high priest is saved forever. This is significant – there can be no fear of death left. Our hope in this high priest is not that he will only fulfill this role for a time or that he is going to disappear, but in fact he has been declared high priest for ever, and therefore he wins salvation forever for those who obey him. The old Aaronic order, of course, with the repeated sacrifices of all those animals, was only for what we might call ceremonial sin, sins of unwitting impurity, sins of an unintentional kind: that was all that the old covenant blood sacrifice could deal with. It could only cleanse someone from an external type of sin, perhaps after touching a dead body – now that was paid for and redeemed (Num 15:22-29). What it could not pay for was wilful, intentional sinning. It never paid for the real sins of the heart; it could never deal with that, ever. Now the once-forever sacrifice of Jesus deals with all sin for all time. Jesus was indeed 'designated by God as high priest in the order of Melchizedek.'

Chapter 5:11-14

11We have much to say about this, but it is hard to explain, because you are dull of hearing. 12Although by this time you ought to be teachers, you need someone to reteach you the basic principles of God's word. You need milk, not solid food!

13For everyone who lives on milk is still an infant, inexperienced in the message of righteousness. 14But solid food is for the mature, who by constant use have trained their senses to distinguish good from evil.

5:11-14 At this point the writer interrupts the argument about Melchizedek and about Jesus the high priest being in a whole new order, which we will pick up again in chapter 7, and he now moves into a warning and application coupled with a strong encouragement. 'We have much to say about this,' the writer is saying, 'about the whole order of Melchizedek and the high priesthood, but it is hard to explain because you are slow to learn, or inattentive. I wish I could tell you more about this, but in fact you need someone to teach you the elementary truths of God's word all over again, even though by this time you ought to be teachers yourselves.' That refers to the basic building blocks of the faith, the ABCs, if you like. The writer is saying 'I have a lot to teach you, but you are just not up to it, you actually need to go back to the ABCs, you need milk, not solid food.' In the scriptures, food is to the body as the word is to the spirit, so the analogy is always about food strengthening the body, and spiritual food providing for the spirit. So how hungry do we need to be; how much do we miss out on all sorts of riches if we are not eating well? Our attitude can be one of 'enough is enough, I read my bible verses this morning, I've done my bit and now I'm too busy.' We will see more about hunger shortly.

Milk is for babies because it is easily digestible, and perhaps for sickly people as well. If you are a baby you cannot digest more solid food, which is for the mature who have grown up. These readers are being likened to babies who cannot cope with solid food and have to take the easy, the superficial, and almost lay a new foundation. What has happened to them?

Is it possible for a believer to go round and round the mountain for years and years and never grow? Is it possible for that to happen for 40 years? Perhaps it happens because milk is received at the breast, where babies have everything done for them, and so we can develop a culture of entitlement, but we will never grow up like that. Our contemporary culture is one of 'grab and go' instant gratification, where we imbibe a spirit of entitlement. In contrast, the mature should be like a weaned child, content (Psa 131:2), rather than always looking for easy gratification and satisfaction at the breast. Solid food is teaching about righteousness, and we shall have to consider what that looks like. Let us contemplate, then, what sort of diet most of God's people get fed on today, and examine the diet of the body of Christ, what we need if we are to grow up and be mature sons and daughters who can cope with suffering, cope with righteous challenges, and emerge as an amazing family – even an army – to meet a world that is profoundly lost.

Hunger

I'm aware in my own life of periods of great spiritual hunger, and then periods when I just don't seem to have any appetite. Such hunger is actually a gift. There is nothing we can boast about in saying that we get hungry, but rather we need to acknowledge that this comes from God. At other times we have to say, 'Lord please will you give me this hunger, I seem to have lost it,' and I believe he graciously gives us back this hunger. Hunger is what makes us reach for the food; it is an appetite instead of a religious duty where we increase the standard of what we do for God. It is not a determination, for example, to have longer times of quiet or of intercession. It is, rather, an appetite inside that yearns: 'I just want to see your face, Jesus,' or a desire to pursue the unsearchable riches of Christ. That isn't hearing again the basic teaching that God loves us – although this teaching is absolutely fundamental and necessary – but it can be a longing to encounter that love in an ever more profound way. There seem to be riches arrayed around for the hungry, for the ones who have an appetite, the diligent, those who say 'I don't want grab and go, instead feed me with more mature things so my heart can grow up more and more in the ways of righteousness, that I might live more and more like a son or a daughter.'

God is delighted with this attitude, and the maturity that follows shines out to others who really need to learn what it is to participate as a marathon runner. It is a long-haul run, and we have this one chance, this one opportunity to run our great marathon for Jesus. Part of how to do this well is seen in how we handle suffering, how we deal with the inevitable knocks in life, so that we don't give up or drift away, because we are feeding ourselves with richer treasure that somehow immovably anchors us, causing us to grow in maturity.

There are people I greatly admire in their Christian walk for their maturity. I watch their poise, and I think 'how do you do that?' I watch them worshipping whilst they are at the bottom of the valley, and I wonder what it is in them that makes that possible. It so inspires me to keep running myself, because I recognise they are anchored so well because they are feeding on solid food, not on baby milk which can be simply the knowledge that 'Jesus loves you.' We all need to know that truth, but not as the *only* source that we are nurtured by. In the natural, if we do not eat, we will feel hungry; if we don't get hungry that is not normal, there is something wrong. Or if we are planning to run a marathon, part of the preparation is the diet: we don't just eat what we like, we eat what we know is healthy and what will help us to run and finish the course. We can ask God to give us more hunger for the right food we need to keep going in our race.

Our appetite and hunger can bring a dissatisfaction with sameness. We can read some scripture passages that really challenge us, making us think 'God, I have not seen that yet in my life, when can I see that happen?' That is appetite, it is not getting frustrated. We can also be thinking about the rest of the body of Christ around us – should our fellow runners in the race have a richer, fuller feeding to cause them to grow up? One of the benefits of working systematically through his word as we are doing here with Hebrews, which does require some effort, is that it does not filter anything out; we come under the full counsel of God, not only the certain parts we love because they give us a bit of a lift. We may love ministering or witnessing to others or hearing about the Father's love, but we also need solid food, the whole word of God, to guard our marathon run from being knocked off course because we became disenchanted, when we didn't understand the fullness of his will.

Prayer

Father, thank you for giving us Jesus as our great high priest, for making a way for us to come back into relationship with you. We ask for grace to grow ever deeper in knowing you as our Father, to have a hunger for more of your presence in our lives, and for a deeper submission of our wills to your way even in the midst of suffering or difficulty. May we know you more intimately every day as our Abba, trusting in your loving care for us in every situation. We ask this through Jesus your Son. Amen.

Questions

Have there been or are there now areas of struggle or suffering in your life, in which God doesn't seem to be present or working as you would like him to? Can you trust him as Abba, enough to say 'not my will but yours'?

Have you experienced times of hungering for more of God? If so, can you see those as precious times of growing in intimacy with him? Would it be good to ask for more hunger now?

Hebrews 6

Persevering in God's promise

Chapter 6:1-6

¹Therefore let us leave the elementary teachings about Christ and go on to maturity, not laying again the foundation of repentance from dead works, and of faith in God, ²instruction about baptisms, the laying on of hands, the resurrection of the dead, and eternal judgment. ³And this we will do, if God permits.

⁴It is impossible for those who have once been enlightened, who have tasted the heavenly gift, who have shared in the Holy Spirit, ⁵who have tasted the goodness of the word of God and the powers of the coming age— ⁶and then have fallen away—to be restored again to repentance, because they themselves are crucifying the Son of God all over again and subjecting Him to open shame.

6:1-3 This passage continues directly from the end of the previous chapter, which has been artificially separated here by the placement of the chapter divisions. We could start by asking ourselves: in this list of elementary teachings, where do we most lack in the foundations that should be laid for all God's people? First on the list is repentance: the power of repentance is crucial to the marathon. Repentance simply means an acknowledgment that this is the wrong way altogether, then forsaking it, turning away from it, and coming right back to the Father's way and being ready to continue on that way. Repentance is very powerful. I have experienced situations when I've been reluctant to repent, and I have experienced times when I've been willing to, and the difference in my journey has been huge. In this context, the writer is probably referring more specifically to repentance from paganism and practices such as idol worship; for us this means turning away from everything in our old life that is not consistent with how our heavenly Father would now want us to live.

Second on the list is faith in God, and we will learn more about that in chapter 11. Next are baptisms. I have been in a number of settings where I felt prompted to ask, 'is everybody here baptised?' It had nothing to do with what I was talking about, and I was in a room full of believers, but there were always hands up indicating that people have not been baptised. Perhaps this is because we often forget to mention it and to encourage people to be baptised. We say to people 'get born again, you are forgiven, the Father loves you' – all true, all true – 'come home, come into the kingdom,' but if they miss out on baptism in water, they miss out on a powerful deliverance from the whole of their old life, that sets them free to start on a new journey, as a new species called a son or a daughter of God.

Baptisms are powerful. Baptism matters! It is part of the actual entrance into the kingdom, because it cuts us off from our whole past. And perhaps we should not wait too long before baptising people – when somebody says 'I want to be baptised' there should be no delay in finding enough water, plunging them under, and cutting them off from their past. The power of baptism can be more evident in some other cultures. In some places in India, people pray the prayer and commit their lives to Jesus, but do not consider themselves Christians until the moment they have been baptised. When they come out of the water they ask 'what is my new name?' because their old name is associated with their old religion, but the new name declares who they have now become. Some non-Christian families will disown new believers as soon as they get baptised – they recognise that something eternal has happened, something that has changed this person.

Next in the list of foundational teachings is the laying on of hands. Putting this alongside the other things here suggests it has greater significance than perhaps some of us have given it, and our understanding of its importance may be limited. Church traditions that maintain the practice of sacramental confirmation may be giving it a more appropriate emphasis. There is something about the laying on of hands that is not just for an impartation of more of the Holy Spirit; God has also ordained it that the laying on of hands by people called to this role is for a commissioning of men and women whom God already owns, to raise them into a level of authority and anointing that they did not have before. This is far more than a ceremonial gesture; it is a powerful efficacious God-kissed laying on of hands to bring authority and anointing. There is more to this than perhaps we have hitherto understood.

We do not often hear preaching or teaching on the resurrection from the dead or eternal judgment. These may seem fearful topics to consider, but in fact they give us an incredibly hopeful, eternal perspective of what it means to be in the marathon we are running. Understanding these topics helps us realise that it is all about an incredible finish where the dead are raised, and we stand before the King of kings for his eternal judgment on the world, but without any fear or feeling of being crushed, because we are following Jesus. Although we are not called to understand exactly how or when, eternal judgment will happen, in an incredibly powerful way.

All these things need to be taught and need to be talked about – yet what kind of diet are God's people getting that should provide a solid basis of truth and revelation, so that they can move on into maturity? Are the foundations of faith being well-laid in the church we see around us? How solid is our understanding of these elementary teachings – are we properly prepared to progress into maturity in our faith?

6:4-6 This is probably one of the most difficult and challenging passages in the New Testament, but it is there and so we need to deal with it. We have encountered the early warnings about drifting away, taking care, staying anchored; then we were encouraged not to harden our hearts, to turn away, or to rebel. Here the writer is talking about those who do fall away or become apostate. The warnings seem to be getting louder, and in fact there is another even louder one to come. But we need to see these in the context of the whole overarching message of Hebrews, which ends with a stunning climax about heaven that should surely make our hearts burn. The warnings get louder not because God wants to say anything like, 'don't think it is that easy, I am going to keep troubling you every now and then just to make sure.' No, it is not like that. The writer is weaving in these warnings because it is a long marathon, and the prize is so huge. Sometimes warnings help us to keep well away from the dangers that might lead us astray.

When my wife and I used to go on family holidays with our children I would love cliff walks, and every now and then we would come across a sign that said 'Warning: cliff erosion.' The sign would often be at least 6 metres away from the cliff edge, as though to say: 'thus far is safe; you can go further, but the further you go the more likely you are to go right off the edge, because there is erosion over there.' The warnings tell us not to go any further off the path, because if we do step nearer the edge, the likelihood of a long fall and a crash greatly increases. Even what looks to be safe ground away from the path may turn out not to be safe after all – keep to the path!

Here the writer is saying that those who have been enlightened, have tasted of the heavenly gift, partaken of the Spirit, tasted the goodness of the word of God, and the powers of the age to come, and who then say 'I turn my back on it, I close the door on it, I will have nothing to do with it,' are crucifying the Son of God all over again, in a way that is shocking. They had received all these gifts, they had belonged to him, but then they said in a public way, 'No, there is no God, I will have nothing to do with this any more.' They were openly denouncing the Son of God, or effectively saying 'I am trampling on all that he has done for me by the shedding of his blood.'

Now obviously the question is: who is this talking about? Is the writer saying that it is impossible for a person to bring themselves to repent because of the way they have lived, but it is always possible for God to save them in his mercy by intervening directly in their lives? Or does it refer to people who have had some taste of but have not totally given their lives over to Jesus, so they are not true believers; they have been skirting around in the periphery of the things of God but have only had some small taste of this life? Or perhaps he is talking about absolutely committed believers, as evidenced by these hallmarks of those who have entered the kingdom: they have tasted the powers, they have tasted the goodness of God's word and they have been transformed by the Spirit.

Is it even referring to those who have been there, experienced the riches of God through Jesus Christ, have given their all to him, but at some point they say 'I'm out;' not just bored, or dispirited because it has all gone horribly wrong, but a flagrant turning of their backs on all they have experienced and a denying that there is any good in it whatsoever? Perhaps we know of people who have left their faith publicly in such a way as to have huge influence on others, for example with a pronouncement that atheism is the way to live. We may not be able to say for certain which of these groups of people the writer had in mind, but in one sense we do not have to come to a clear conclusion, because whichever it is, it should make us tremble a bit, and be absolutely diligent to anchor ourselves in what matters most.

If we take all the warnings of the New Testament, of which there are a number, we have to give credence to the possibility that we cannot guarantee we will persevere to the end. We may not be able to hold to the saying 'Once saved, always saved.' No one can make the judgment except God himself, and of course we are not called to judge another person's salvation. Nonetheless, perhaps we need these warnings to keep away from the edge: warnings that make our hearts tremble, not with fear of what God might do to us, but with an awesome reverential submission, because we know they will protect us in our journey. The danger of holding to the position of 'Once saved, always saved' is complacency; we may think we have ticked a box and achieved something. It allows us, especially those less mature who have not trained their senses, to take on an attitude towards life in which we lose a sense of awe towards God, where we are unaware that we have to hold a tension between the love of the Father and the true biblical fear of the Lord of the universe, yet not the fear of punishment – there is a world of difference between these two.

Chapter 6:7-12

7For land that drinks in the rain often falling on it and that produces a crop useful to those for whom it is tended receives the blessing of God.

89

8But land that produces thorns and thistles is worthless, and its curse is imminent. In the end it will be burned.

9Even though we speak like this, beloved, we are convinced of better things in your case—things that accompany salvation. 10For God is not unjust. He will not forget your work and the love you have shown for His name as you have ministered to the saints and continue to do so.

11We want each of you to show this same diligence to the very end, in order to make your hope sure. 12Then you will not be sluggish, but will imitate those who through faith and patience inherit what has been promised.

6:7-8 The land that drinks in the rain refers to our hearts. The writer has been talking about the condition of our hearts: 'Today, if you hear His voice, do not harden your hearts' (Psa 95:7-8). The land that often drinks the rain is a heart that is thirsty or hungry – we are back to the hunger again – which is one of the ways we can be sure to avoid falling away, to be diligent so that we never even get near to the warning sign. We want to stay away from the sign, let alone what is beyond the sign; we want to be so firmly on the path that we remain far away from the sign, even though we might drift near it once or twice in our marathon. When the land drinks in the rain, this causes fruitfulness to spring up, because our hearts are softened. Such tender hearts drink easily, whilst the rain rebounds off hardened hearts. This is a similar image to the parable of the sower (Matt 13:1-9): when the seed falls on the path or the rocky places, or among the thorns and the thistles and the cares of life, the land is not drinking in or receiving these glorious seeds that make our heart come alive. But the good soil, which is the noble heart, by persevering, produces a hundred-fold crop. The writer is highlighting that our hearts can be like land that drinks in the rain often falling on it and produces a manifold crop, but can also be hardened by not drinking in the rain, producing thorns and thistles.

6:9-12 After that rebuke and warning, we now move on to the great encouragement that follows: the writer addresses his readers as 'beloved' again. In this passage about work and diligence, God is not saying 'because you have so loved God's people and done your best in serving them, your salvation is now secure: welcome to the end.' That would be a works-based thought again, that because we did our best for his people, we have somehow earned the final prize. The writer is not talking about striving to make our salvation clear or to produce a crop in order to receive the blessing of God: 'Therefore, brothers, be all the more eager to make your calling and election sure. For if you practise these things you will never stumble' (2 Pet 1:10). Rather than striving, we are encouraged to make every effort by being diligent and hungry, not lazy or complacent or a little hardened, by constantly pursuing everything God says to us, not letting it pass by in a passive superficiality and a false sense of security – and by doing that we will receive blessing. Perhaps we need to repent of any sense that we are looking for someone else to give us what we need on earth, when we should be pursuing for ourselves what the high priest himself wants to give to us.

In fact, the writer wants to tell us that the 'better things' that accompany salvation are the fruit of someone whose life has been given to Jesus, and so their whole passion is to help God's people, to help others, to raise them up and aid them on their journey. That is the fruit of a heart that is tender, and is part of God's fathering agenda for us. It is not a list of all the good things someone did, which God will remember at the end of time when they make it to the end of the journey, run through the finishing tape and are therefore allowed into his presence. It is not that; they are the things that *accompany* salvation.

If however none of those things is present, then it is reasonable to wonder where somebody is at in their journey with the Lord. 'What good is it, my brothers, if someone claims to have faith, but has no deeds? Can such faith save him?' (James 2:14). If there is no external expression or evidence, if there is no working out of faith so that those who were meant to serve and help actually do so, we might wonder where their heart is orientated. All the writer is saying is that God is looking at those things, and if we have sown there will be some form of reaping that God has intended for us, that somehow crowns us and blesses us in addition to our being safely saved. That is quite encouraging: it means we must keep going, not get lazy, and imitate those who through faith and patience inherit the promise, and we will see blessing in our lives. And who is it that inherits? Not servants or slaves, not orphans, but sons and daughters.

In his letter to the Galatians, Paul writes 'Do not be deceived: God cannot be mocked. Whatever a man sows, he will reap in return' (Gal 6:7). But what does it mean to be mocked? What we sow into the spirit we definitely reap – we do experience blessing from God when we put him first and seek to follow him in obedience; when we sow into the flesh by following our own desires we will reap eternal destruction. It is not that 'God cannot be mocked' in the sense that we get what we expected from what we sow, no – rather he is moved by our compassion for others, especially where we have sowed with tears, so that we receive far more than we had anticipated.

He is so moved that he says to us, 'I guarantee to you wherever you sow into the spirit you will reap life, even if it takes time to see it. It is guaranteed.' Just as it is guaranteed that if we sow into our flesh, we feel something of the separation of death afterwards, in the same way it is as if God is saying, 'I have seen the way you gave with tears, and I reward it even though it has nothing to do with your salvation.' God's people need reassuring sometimes with the certainty of reaping when they have sowed in tears; even when we have done this in secret and no one has seen, the Lord says 'I didn't miss it. That principle can never be mocked, I'm the one who gave that principle. You will reap.' We can therefore trust in the truth that 'God is not unjust. He will not forget your work and the love you have shown for His name as you have ministered to the saints and continue to do so' (6:10).

Chapter 6:13-20

13When God made His promise to Abraham, since He had no one greater to swear by, He swore by Himself, 14saying, "I will surely bless you and multiply your descendants." 15And so Abraham, after waiting patiently, obtained the promise.

16Men swear by someone greater than themselves, and their oath serves as a confirmation to end all argument. 17So when God wanted to make the unchanging nature of His purpose very clear to the heirs of the promise, He guaranteed it with an oath. *18Thus by two unchangeable things in which it is impossible for God to lie, we who have fled to take hold of the hope set before us may be strongly encouraged.*

19We have this hope as an anchor for the soul, firm and steadfast. It enters the inner sanctuary behind the curtain, 20where Jesus our forerunner has entered on our behalf. He has become a high priest forever in the order of Melchizedek.

6:13-15 Here is one of the themes of Hebrews: through faith and patience we are guaranteed to inherit what God promises. We need more faith and more patience. The writer has encouraged us to imitate those who have already received their inheritance, as a provocation to us to keep going in the marathon, to trust God in our journey, and he now gives us the example of Abraham. The promises to Abraham are, first: 'You will be the father of many nations' (Gen 17:4), and secondly: 'I will surely bless you, and I will multiply your descendants like the stars in the sky and the sand on the seashore' (Gen 22:17) – God chooses such outrageous images, things that are impossible to count or to even conceive the number. The third promise is: 'Through your offspring all nations of the earth will be blessed' (Gen 22:18), and the fourth, 'To you and your descendants I will give the land of your sojourn – all the land of Canaan – as an eternal possession' (Gen 17:8). After waiting patiently, Abraham received what was promised.

In order to have a line of descendants, Abraham needed to have a son, but it was a long time between the first promise and its fulfillment, twenty-five years in fact. The very first hint of the promise is given immediately after God's call to Abraham to leave his country. He says, 'I will make you into a great nation, and I will bless you; I will make your name great, so that you will be a blessing. I will bless those who bless you and curse those who curse you; and all the families of the earth will be blessed through you... Abram was seventy-five years old when he left Haran' (Gen 12:2-4). This promise was given to Abraham, it settled into his heart, and then he began a journey of faith and patience. He needed patience because there was no sign of the fulfillment and he was getting older. He needed patience because everything about the situation was getting increasingly impossible: his body was 'decrepit' (Rom 4:19), and his wife was long past the age of child bearing – in her 90s (Gen 17:17). Yet, the promise *was* eventually fulfilled: Sarah 'bore a son to Abraham in his old age, at the very time God had promised him' (Gen 21:2); 'Abraham was a hundred years old when his son Isaac was born to him' (Gen 21:5).

Twenty-five years is a long time to wait. Abraham is the model from whom we can draw great inspiration, because many of us have heard promises, things that came into our hearts which we really thought would happen within a certain time frame, but didn't. Maybe then even more time passed, and they still had not happened, and then it seemed more and more impossible until it was definitely impossible, and it *still* had not happened. So in the marathon run we are learning about, it is as if the Lord is saying, 'Do not give up! Just because you have not seen it happen, it doesn't mean I have forgotten you, do not withdraw, do not drift away; look at Abraham as a magnificent model of faith and patience.' Now of course we remember that in fact he wasn't perfect in this: he tried to bring about the promise himself through his wife's servant Hagar (Gen 16:1-4); and that doesn't look much like patience. He questioned God's ability to fulfill the promise and he tried to persuade God to give his blessing to his illegitimate son Ishmael instead (Gen 17:17-18). Yet Abraham's whole journey, despite his human frailties, is meant to inspire us that it is through faith and also through patience that God's promises are fulfilled. Patience is thus very important.

In my own family I have been praying for more than twenty years for a miraculous healing. Should I persevere, or do I back down, accept the situation and do my best to journey with it? The dimension of miracle needed seems to get greater, but equally so should my faith: we go from faith to more faith, the levels are always rising because there is no end to the increase of his kingdom. Sometimes we can get discouraged and some part of our faith inside us subtly comes down a notch, and we think 'I'm not going to do that, I'll just cope with it now, because I don't want to get my hopes up and then fall back on my face again.' Many of us have these situations, but if we do not keep our hearts tender then the hardening begins, and we can start to say, 'don't talk about those things with me, it is too painful.' We may have seen enough to encourage us that God is able to do astonishing things, amazing signs and wonders, but we need to be honest with ourselves about the level of our faith because we don't want to get hardened in our hearts, but neither do we want to be hurt by another disappointment. What is key here is that every disappointment can be another diminishing of the longer-term journey and the call to faith and patience.

It is patience that can be most challenging for us in these situations. Patience can have the meaning 'abiding under,' or staying fixed or anchored while being tested. Navigating these really testing things and holding on with faith and patience is challenging, but we can look to Abraham who just did it honestly like all of us would. We might start to think: 'do we need to try a 'Hagar' alternative? What will do it?' But the Lord says 'No, I have to take you right through this time of difficulty,' because at some point Abraham and Sarah became ready for the fulfillment of the promise in a way that they had clearly not been before. There is a principle of journeying here. This journey through faith and patience to inheriting the promises God has made to us, when perhaps we are in deep and personal pain, wanting to withdraw but deciding we are not going to, is a vital part of growing in sonship and daughterhood, of a deepening trust in the true fathering of our eternal Father in heaven.

6:16-18 'God is not a man, that He should lie, or a son of man, that He should change his mind' (Num 23:19). Men swear by someone greater than themselves – they might swear by the king or the queen, declaring: 'as surely as the king is king, it will happen; I promise you by the name of the king if it does not happen, he is no longer the king.' The oath confirms what is said and puts an end to all argument about it. Because God wanted to make the unchanging nature of his purpose very clear to us, who are the heirs of what was promised, he confirmed the promise with an oath.

The 'two unchangeable things' are these: God is the only person in the whole universe that when he says something, it always happens. There is no doubt and he does not change his mind. In addition, in this case of the high priesthood, the work of Jesus Christ, and us being heirs, he actually seals this with an oath – not that he should ever have to because his word is his word – but in his compassion for us, to give us a deep anchor to hold onto, he adds an oath and says, 'I promise.' The oath confirms that if it does not happen, then God is not God. He cannot swear by anybody higher, because there is nobody greater than God himself, so he swears by himself in the sense that 'I promise you, and if it does not happen I'm no longer God.' Thus, he gives his word and he swears an oath, and by these two unchangeable things, we who have fled the whole world and anchored our hope in him may be deeply reassured of the certainty of his promise.

6:19-20 The huge chain that holds the anchor to a ship is what secures it against all storms. The picture here is that as we completely trust in all God has given us, there is an anchor chained to our hearts that goes right through the curtain into the holy of holies, where the great high priest is there on our behalf. We note that the anchor was an early Christian symbol for hope in the future life, adopted in the times of Roman persecution and commonly found in the ancient catacombs today. The chain anchors our hearts right into that holy of holies and secures our hearts, so that as the storms come, we are held so firmly in hope by two unchangeable things, secured and utterly unmovable.

Under the Old Covenant the high priest went in behind the curtain of the tabernacle once a year for the cleansing ceremony (Lev 16). This was a remarkable time; but what was it like going in to the holy of holies? What would happen as he entered the presence of God? Everybody stood outside in a nervous awe wondering whether the high priest would ever come out. According to a Jewish legend from the middle ages, they would tie a scarlet rope around his ankle so that if he stayed too long, they could pull him out, in case he was being burned up by the presence of God. With Jesus as our high priest, however, we are tied to him by our belief in his promise, our hearts anchored to him as he is there on our behalf, and this firm and secure hope means he can actually pull us in with him to the holy of holies. He has entered before the throne of God as the forerunner, and we are going to follow after him into the presence of the Father. When storms come, then, we are absolutely steadied and anchored to Jesus the high priest, because of the certain hope that we have in God's promise.

Sometimes we may have found our hearts have become withdrawn, a little hardened, perhaps with a slight loss of hope underlying it all. Here the Lord wants to re-anchor our hearts so that we can be strong runners in the marathon, who through faith and patience are imitators of Abraham the father of the faith: he who so pleased God by daring to stand apart from the struggles of life and say, 'I'm still here Lord, and I want to run all the way, I do not want to have a heart that is withdrawn or hardened.' Therefore, as we continue our journey through the word, the Holy Spirit may want to revitalise us again and wipe away some of the weariness of unfulfilled promise, whether in a specific situation or just in the profound state of being a true pilgrim. Let us pray that God will release upon us hope and patience from the Holy Spirit, which will truly anchor us.

Prayer

Father, we need you to make what we are reading about real and tangible. We ask you to wash away dust and wounds and bruising from every heart, and renew in us a deepening faith and patience to keep on in the journey, knowing that we can utterly rely on what you say to us. Where hope has been diminished by blows, by hurts or disappointments, breathe on our trusting hearts. Let that big rope which anchors us to your Son be tied firmly in place. Amen.

Questions

How solid are the foundations of your faith? Are there 'idols' that you need to turn away from? Have you been baptised? Have you ever had somebody lay hands on you to pray for authority and anointing on your life?

Is there anything you have needed to wait for with patience, that God has yet to fulfill? Does your hope and trust in God's promise sometimes need renewing? If so, how can you do this?

Hebrews 7

The priesthood of Jesus is far superior

After the diversion of the latest strong warning followed by a great encouragement, we are now returning to Melchizedek and the ongoing comparison of Jesus' high priesthood being far superior to the old Aaronic one. Although that may not mean a huge amount to us, for the Jews it was such a big change in thinking that the writer was working to establish – just as it was for Peter on the roof (Acts 10). In addition, there are some insights for us here concerning the nature of Jesus' high priesthood: he is king as well as high priest.

Chapter 7:1-10

¹This Melchizedek was king of Salem and priest of God Most High. He met Abraham returning from the slaughter of the kings and blessed him, ²and Abraham apportioned to him a tenth of everything. First, his name means "king of righteousness." Then also, "king of Salem" means "king of peace." ³Without father or mother or genealogy, without beginning of days or end of life, like the Son of God, he remains a priest for all time.

⁴Consider how great Melchizedek was: Even the patriarch Abraham gave him the first tenth of the plunder. ⁵Now the law commands the sons of Levi who become priests to collect a tenth from the people—that is, from their brothers—though they too are descended from Abraham. ⁶But Melchizedek, who did not trace his descent from Levi, collected a tenth from Abraham and blessed him who had the promises. ⁷And indisputably, the lesser is blessed by the greater.

⁸In the case of the Levites, mortal men collect the tenth; but in the case of Melchizedek, it is affirmed that he lives on. ⁹And so to speak, Levi, who collects the tenth, paid the tenth through Abraham. ¹⁰For when Melchizedek met Abraham, Levi was still in the loin of his ancestor.

7:1-3 This Melchizedek is a mysterious figure, who appeared in the time of the patriarchs, a long time before Levi and Aaron, and is mentioned briefly in Genesis 14:18-20. Abraham had been to war and had returned after winning a great victory. When Abraham came back two things happened: Melchizedek blessed Abraham, and Abraham gave a tithe to him. The writer to the Hebrews tells us a few things about Melchizedek, and we need to understand the relevance of these. First, he has no genealogy, no identified father or mother, no family tree, which contrasts strongly with the Aaronic order which is all to do with genealogy, and where your only right to be there is as a descendent of Aaron and Levi. Secondly, he has no documented beginning or end, so he lives forever. Thirdly, his name means king of peace and king of righteousness, and he is both a king and a priest, so he combines these two elements of the kingdom. Both his kingship and his priesthood are about peace and righteousness. In this way, he is the anticipation of the joining of those two roles in the person of Jesus Christ himself, who is a king-priest of the ultimate kind. Lastly, 'he remains a priest for all time,' so he is an eternal priest.

So who was Melchizedek? Was he a real historical figure? We do not know, but in fact, this doesn't really matter, because Jewish thinking was less interested in the detail of historical facts, and much more interested in the allegorical meaning of what those facts could teach them, to learn more about God. Although most likely he was a real person who simply did not have any records of his parenthood, and so was said not to have a mother or father, the Holy Spirit uses the facts of whoever he was to highlight some really important qualities about a whole new order of priesthood. He is an eternal priest who does not come from a genealogical line of priests.

7:4-10 In the Levitical order, the Levites would normally collect the tithes from the people, symbolizing how the Levites were greater than the people (because tithes are paid to those greater than the person paying them), and the Levites would then in turn bless the people. That is the Aaronic order of things. In this case, however, before the Aaronic order ever came about, a higher order of priesthood is foreseen when Melchizedek meets with Abraham. Abraham tithes to Melchizedek and Melchizedek blesses Abraham. Here, the writer to the Hebrews encourages the reader to consider just how great he was, that even the patriarch Abraham gave a tenth of the plunder to him. He goes on to say, with regard to the Levitical order, that it could be considered that Levi was also in effect tithing to Melchizedek, as he was in the loins of Abraham. The point he wants the Jewish believers to understand is this: although the Aaronic order of priesthood was powerful, how far greater and superior is the whole new order coming out of Melchizedek.

Tithing

It would be better if we could avoid talking about tithing, wouldn't it? As followers of Jesus, many give away a tenth of their income simply because they have been taught that this is the right thing to do. Others consider it a legalistic Old Testament practice that we are now free from under the New Covenant, and there would be no trouble in believing this if we avoided the fact that tithing first happened *before* the law, when there was no law, and Abraham voluntarily tithed the plunder to someone greater than he who was in the order of the coming Son of God. That idea of tithing was so profound, that it has persisted as an eternal pointer to the willing release of our first fruits to God, and it still points towards something very significant, but without putting some kind of a mandatory 'God-tax' on us all. It remains significant here, because without it we could easily think that tithing is just part of being under the law, and now we are free from the law, so we can be grateful that we do not have to do this any more.

Yet, that occasion in Genesis 14 is very moving, with that willing surrender of the first fruits to someone of a greater order. It seems to imply that there is something about tithing which was never meant to become a kind of 'tax' on believers, but it is significant for a New Testament people who delight in giving their first fruits to God in some way. Tithing should be talked about again amongst God's people, because there was in the past a reaction to the legalistic side of it, and like a lot of reactions it went too far in the other direction, obscuring the truth that there may be something very beautiful at the heart of it that was meant to bring great life and release to us.

The Aaronic priesthood required men to be of that lineage and was limited to those aged between twenty or twenty-five and fifty (1 Chron 23:24-27; Num 8:23-16). They had at most thirty years of service and then they had to make way. It was a constantly revolving priesthood of a frail human kind, giving service for a time, that was then over. The priesthood of Melchizedek that preceded this, before the law was given, before Levi and Aaron, was radically different, and retains a degree of mystery, hinting at the future – for example he 'brought out bread and wine' (Gen 14:18) points to Jesus' offering of bread and wine at the last supper (Matt 26:26-29). Everything about Melchizedek is a type, a shadow of the fullness to come. The beauty of the person of Melchizedek is that he is all about promise and not law. Jesus is king of peace and righteousness and a high priest in the order of Melchizedek.

Chapter 7:11-16

11Now if perfection could have been attained through the Levitical priesthood (for on this basis the people received the law), why was there still need for another priest to appear—one in the order of Melchizedek and not in the order of Aaron? 12For when the priesthood is changed, the law must be changed as well.

13He of whom these things are said belonged to a different tribe, from which no one has ever served at the altar. 14For it is clear that our Lord descended from Judah, a tribe as to which Moses said nothing about priests.

15 And this point is even more clear if another priest like Melchizedek appears, 16 one who has become a priest not by a law of succession, but by the power of an indestructible life.

7:11-16 The Old Covenant was so deeply ingrained in Jewish belief as being the ultimate answer, with the priesthood and the sacrifices, the law and the temple worship, that they struggled with the idea it was about to be brought to a conclusion by a completely different order. They found it hard not to carry some of the old order over into their new faith. In fact, the thought of closing the era of the Old Covenant was quite disturbing to the Jewish believers; we see an example of this in Acts 15, where they were still trying to carry over the practice of circumcision. Perfection had been measured by adherence to the law, and the old Levitical priesthood was adequate to ensure this, and was in fact designed to bring this about. But this law had now been superseded. In fact the law was only ever meant to be a temporary guardian 'to lead us to Christ, that we might be justified by faith. Now that faith has come, we are no longer under a guardian' (Gal 3:24-25). So if the law had been replaced by something greater, a new priesthood was also needed to bring that about.

We are very aware of the ability of empty religion to deny the absolute power of the blood of Jesus to free us completely into righteousness, so it is easier for us to say 'No, we don't want to carry unnecessary things over from the old into the new.' For the Jews it was much more of a struggle. A new law and a new priesthood were needed; the priesthood would be from a different lineage and hence be a different kind of priesthood altogether, and this would be for all time. Jesus is high priest 'by the power of an indestructible life,' just as Melchizedek had no documented beginning or end.

Chapter 7:17-25

17 For it is testified:

"You are a priest forever

in the order of Melchizedek."

18So the former commandment is set aside because it was weak and useless 19(for the law made nothing perfect), and a better hope is introduced, by which we draw near to God.

20And none of this happened without an oath. For others became priests without an oath, 21but Jesus became a priest with an oath by the One who said to Him:

"The Lord has sworn and will not change His mind:
'You are a priest forever.'"

22Because of this oath, Jesus has become the guarantee of a better covenant.

23Now there have been many other priests, since death prevented them from continuing in office. 24But because Jesus lives forever, He has a permanent priesthood. 25Therefore He is able to save completely those who draw near to God through Him, since He always lives to intercede for them.

7:17-19 Verse 17 quotes Psalm 110:4, affirming the eternal nature of the priesthood of Christ, clearly different from the transience of the Aaronic priesthood. Under the Old Covenant it was in many ways very simple: as long as a man keeps the law, he is a friend of God. Here is the priesthood, there is the law: if you keep the law you are a friend of God, and you have absolute access to his close friendship, the door is wide open. However, mankind is unable to keep all the requirements of the law, and therefore the access to God is blocked; the sacrifices of the priests that in the Old Testament only covered the external, ceremonial and unclean sin, cannot solve the problem of access back to God because of personal, internal sin.

In Romans 8:3 we read, 'For what the law was powerless to do in that it was weakened by the flesh, God did by sending His own Son in the likeness of sinful man, as an offering for sin.' The law was good, God-given, but 'the former commandment is set aside because it was weak and useless (for the law made nothing perfect).' The Aaronic regulations were absolutely fine for those who kept the law, but as soon as they didn't keep the law it was weak and useless, because it could not deal with the issue of sin. It was unable to give us back the true access to God in our hearts, it just dealt with the external, ceremonial things. It allowed God to dwell amongst them, but without intimate access to him. Through the high priest Jesus and his own sacrifice, a whole new hope is opened up that is completely different to any hope the Aaronic priesthood could ever offer. The result is simple: we can draw near to God again; we can come close to him.

7:20-22 What is the significance of the oath? Why would it mean so much that there was an oath attached to Jesus' priesthood? The oath demonstrates that it is final, permanent and will never be changed. The Hebrews have been used to priests changing every 30 years, and the whole system at its most fundamental lacking the power and ability to achieve the aim of intimate, personal access to God. Then the king is appointed as a high priest and the Father makes an oath over him: 'I will not change my mind, for the whole of eternity, my Son is now high priest forever.' What does that do for human beings? It gives them a level of hope and assurance they can never have in the old order. This is forever, because the Lord has sworn, and if he breaks his promise, he is no longer God.

God is asking us if we will understand. He is predicating his whole nature on this. He is stamping the high priesthood with his heavenly signet ring that says 'I will not change my mind, so that every man and woman can realise deep down that once that anchor of hope has gone out from your heart into the inner of inners, the promise can never be broken, because the Lord will never change his mind.' The attachment of an oath is therefore a striking change of perspective for the people. This never happened with the Aaronic priests because they would die. Jesus is the guarantee of the covenant promise – a far better covenant.

7:23-25 There is now an absolute permanence to this. Jesus' high priesthood is not only of the order of Melchizedek, it is backed by the Father's oath. It is eternal, unlike the successive priests of the old order, because Jesus has an indestructible life; it is forever. It is also all-sufficient, because he has taken everything we need upon himself so that he can become all-sufficient to us.

As our high priest and mediator, Jesus 'lives forever, He has a permanent priesthood' – but what does this mean, that Jesus as a priest is interceding for us? In fact he is continually interceding for us, all the time, without ceasing. The king, after he made purification for sin, sat down at the right hand of the majesty on high as though his work was completely finished. Now if we go into heaven in our imaginations, the king, the high priest, is seated on his throne and intercedes for us, that we might have access to the Father. It is as if Jesus has his blood on his hands as he sits in the Father's presence: 'if anyone does sin, we have an advocate before the Father – Jesus Christ, the Righteous One. He Himself is the atoning sacrifice for our sins' (1 John 2:1-2). In this way, we are allowed permanent access to the Father of the most intimate, continuous, unstoppable and confident kind, because the blood that was shed is on the hands of the king high priest, on our behalf. Jesus has died once for all as a sacrifice to deal with our sin, which had prevented our access to the Father.

Jesus is not standing before a reluctant God and pleading 'Oh please Father, accept them,' but rather God is welcoming us in because he knows we are his; our sin is covered by the blood of Jesus. 'In Him and through faith in Him we may enter God's presence with boldness and confidence' (Eph 3:12). We don't only just about squeeze into the presence of God, but we can come with boldness and freedom forever; the blood of Jesus has done that for us in a way no other blood sacrifice could ever do. It is permanent, it is all-sufficient, it has an oath attached to it so it will never be changed. No words are necessary from Jesus; just him being in the presence of the Father is the intercession. Jesus' interceding is not the same as what we do when interceding, asking, pleading – it is in a different order than our prayer, a different kind of action just by being in the Father's presence. He has paid the price for our sin, and now he sits at the right hand of the Father, and somehow his eternal presence there constitutes his intercession to the Father.

This king and high priest is so deeply *for* us in our journey that we may not always realise just how much he wants to encourage and support us as we run our race. It is as if there is something in heaven that is championing us as we go through life, even – or especially – in the times we experience being hounded by the enemy with accusations or condemnation. But 'Who is there to condemn us? For Christ Jesus, who died, and more than that was raised to life, is at the right hand of God – and He is interceding for us. Who shall separate us from the love of Christ?' (Rom 8:34-35). It is so good to have such a champion in heaven on our personal behalf, having this king cheering us on to endure right to the end, because nothing can separate us from his love. There may even be times when it seems the king himself stands up on our behalf and his standing up seems to cause such a strength behind us, that we overcome in a situation when we might not otherwise have done so. Jesus intercedes on our behalf; he is our advocate, our legal certainty of access before the Father, so that nothing can separate us from his love.

Priesthood

We should note that in the Old Testament era, covenants with God were often made through intermediaries or priests. For example, the people were afraid and said to Moses: 'you talk to God, we don't want to do it, you go and find out what he wants' (see Exod 20:18-19). God was offering a relationship with his people, so these fears were not a good start to the agreement; the Lord wanted more than that for them. When we are considering priesthood now, we should rejoice in the wonder that we no longer need a priest on earth ever again, in any form, to perform that kind of function for us. God has finished with human priesthood as intermediaries, and any tendency in God's people to rely on someone else to go to God for them is foreign to the New Covenant. Whether this is somebody ordained as a priest or someone we rely on because their connection with the Lord seems better than ours, and we think that maybe they could do a little bit of the process for us, it negates the power of the blood of Jesus in winning for us all an absolutely confident and free access to the Lord himself.

There can be an empty, religious pattern of thinking that has grown up around us and which we have perhaps unconsciously taken in, that declares there are some people who have better access to God, upon whom we can lean or depend, but which is utterly foreign to the New Covenant. The role of a priest in Christian ministry therefore is something completely other than a continuation of the Old Covenant idea of priesthood as a mediator, which came to its fulfillment and conclusion in Jesus. It is important for us to work to understand what this role is, so that there is no confusion in our hearts about the role of Jesus as our eternal and only high priest.

Chapter 7:26-28

26Such a high priest truly befits us—One who is holy, innocent, undefiled, set apart from sinners, and exalted above the heavens. 27Unlike the other high priests, He does not need to offer daily sacrifices, first for His own sins and then for the sins of the people; He sacrificed for sin once for all when He offered up Himself. 28For the law appoints as high priests men who are weak; but the oath, which came after the law, appointed the Son, who has been made perfect forever.

7:26 This new high priesthood gives us access, it is permanent; such a high priest truly meets our need, he is our champion, he is all-sufficient for our need personally as the high priest. One who is holy, he is other, he is blameless, he is pure – far surpassing what the Old Testament priesthood required in ritual external purity – he is set apart from sinners and he is exalted above the heavens. We can imagine that the Jews were thinking 'this is not like any high priest we have ever heard of, what does this mean?' He was something other than their expectation; this was such a different order of priesthood that they could not understand what was being described. The writer is pressing the case again and again for the Jews to understand the point that the Aaronic order is obsolete.

7:27-28 Unlike previous priests, there is no need for Jesus to offer regular sacrifices for his own sin, or for the people. There is never a need for another sacrifice again; and there is never a need for us to offer one tiniest bit of extra effort to make sure the sacrifice is sufficient. It was done, it is all-sufficient, and every time we try to add to it by further sacrifice, we are heading back to 'works of death' (9:14). If there is a joy and a freedom, it is that in Jesus, and through faith in him and the work he has done, we may approach God with boldness and freedom and confidence. These commodities in a relationship are very special. There is something about the work he has done that can cause our hearts to come to a level of freedom and confidence in our life of fellowship with him, which is really important when the enemy tries to lie to us. Freedom means we run easily into God's presence. In freedom and confidence, we enter without hesitation, the door is constantly open, there is no reserve because the king and high priest is already there saying, 'come on in, I did it all for you, there is nothing further to be done.'

In summary, this is the comparison of the two priesthoods, showing that Jesus' priesthood is far superior to that of the Old Covenant because of the nature of his priesthood, and because of who he is in himself. Foreshadowed by Melchizedek, Jesus is of a different lineage to the Old Covenant priesthood, in fact he comes from the lineage of kings, and he is holy, blameless, and does not need to offer sacrifices for himself. He lives for ever, intercedes for us for ever, and gains us access to the Father. His sacrifice is permanent, and it is all-sufficient: it deals with every kind of sin. He is the fulfillment of the Levitical priesthood; he truly does meet our need.

Prayer

Father, as we come under the truth of this word, we ask that we will be deeply assured by the power of your Son's blood and his eternal high priesthood. We pray it will give us remarkable confidence and freedom to enjoy our closeness with you, whatever is going on around us. Increase our confidence and freedom to enjoy you, Father, and may condemnation never keep us apart from you when we have confessed our sin. We ask this in Jesus' name. Amen.

Questions

Are there times when you feel condemned, and unable or unworthy to come into the presence of God? What does this chapter say in response to those situations?

Have you ever thought that complete forgiveness is not possible because your sin is too great or too difficult for the blood of Jesus to deal with, even though that might be sufficient for everybody else? What is the truth?

Hebrews 8

The priesthood of Jesus inaugurates the new covenant

Chapter 8:1-6

[1]The point of what we are saying is this: We do have such a high priest, who sat down at the right hand of the throne of the Majesty in heaven, [2]and who ministers in the sanctuary and true tabernacle set up by the Lord, not by man. [3]And since every high priest is appointed to offer both gifts and sacrifices, it was necessary for this One also to have something to offer.

[4]Now if He were on earth, He would not be a priest, since there are already priests who offer gifts according to the law. [5]The place where they serve is a copy and shadow of what is in heaven. This is why Moses was warned when he was about to build the tabernacle: "See to it that you make everything according to the pattern shown you on the mountain."

[6]Now, however, Jesus has received a much more excellent ministry, just as the covenant He mediates is better and is founded on better promises.

Having concluded the comparison between the old Levitical priesthood and that of Jesus, the writer now moves on in the light of that to make two more comparisons. First, the temporary, earthly tabernacle or the subsequent temple in Jerusalem is contrasted with the eternal, true, heavenly one. He then compares the Old Covenant established through Moses on Mount Sinai to the New Covenant brought by Jesus. In each case, the old foreshadowed the new, and now the old has found its fulfillment in the new. The earthly tabernacle had to be built according to the pattern of the 'real' tabernacle (Exod 25:40); what had appeared to be the true place for worship for the people of God has turned out to be a mere shadow of something far more profound and real, the sanctuary where Jesus is seated at the right hand of the Father.

The writer has therefore brought before us a number of comparison statements: in this new era the high priest and his ministry are superior; the place where he carries out his role as mediator is superior; the covenant made is superior; and the promises spoken of or attached to that covenant are also superior. That is a profound summary of what we have been brought into by Jesus.

8:1-2 The writer is summing up the last few chapters where he has introduced these profound truths, and there are more riches still to be uncovered which will deepen our rootedness to Jesus. What we do know is that Jesus is the magnificent, true king-priest, who has sat down at the right side of the throne, signifying the absolute completion of the work he had to do, never forgetting that the three greatest words that are at the pivot of history are what he said at the cross: 'It is finished' (John 19:30). That is profound, there is nothing further to be done, there is no more, there is no going back on it. 'It is finished' is the whole foundation of all that is being discussed here; the work has been done at the cross, and this most decisive moment in the whole of history from the beginning of creation to when Jesus Christ returns is what releases everything we are reading about here. And thus because of that one sacrifice he ministers permanently in the sanctuary, not one day each year, nor in the copy but in the real sanctuary, the true tabernacle. This is such a constant comfort for us, that somehow in his serving he never ceases for a second to represent us with his blood before the throne of God. This is a powerful second-by-second ministry of this true high priest.

8:3-4 Every high priest offers a sacrifice on behalf of those he is representing, but Jesus offers himself, instead of an animal as in the Old Testament. Neither was he part of the Levitical priesthood, the Aaronic order; he did not belong to that tribe or lineage.

8:5-6 Everything about the earthly sanctuary in the Old Testament was a copy and shadow of the true one in heaven. When we read that Jesus passed through the heavens, we should consider that he passed through to the true tabernacle in heaven, and that is why Moses' instructions about the tabernacle were so specific and prophetic, because they foreshadowed the coming reality that Jesus would move into. Jesus takes us from the copy or shadow of what was given to Moses to the fulfillment and substance of what that copy is made from.

A copy or a shadow are never the real thing, they just give us an inkling about the real thing. The whole Old Testament sacrificial system, with its tabernacle, was only a pointer to some incredible reality that you and I would be engaged with through the blood of Christ. And so all of this gives us a shame-free and bold access to an intimate relationship with our Father that only Jesus' blood could accomplish. I love the thought of shame-free boldness: there is no reason to hesitate, to hold back, to fear, or to hide. It means we really are able to come into the presence of the Father in a way that was impossible under the Old Covenant, and this is nothing to do with our behaviour, but solely through the power of Jesus' sacrifice. His ministry mediates a New Covenant that is superior and releases better promises; the old is now obsolete.

Chapter 8:7-13

7For if that first covenant had been without fault, no place would have been sought for a second. 8But God found fault with the people and said:

"Behold, the days are coming, declares the Lord,
*   when I will make a new covenant*
with the house of Israel
*   and with the house of Judah.*
9It will not be like the covenant
*   I made with their fathers*
when I took them by the hand
*   to lead them out of the land of Egypt,*
because they did not abide by My covenant,
*   and I disregarded them,*
declares the Lord.

10For this is the covenant I will make
*   with the house of Israel*

113

> *after those days,*
> > *declares the Lord.*
> *I will put My laws in their minds,*
> > *and inscribe them on their hearts.*
> *And I will be their God,*
> > *and they will be My people.*
> *11No longer will each one teach his neighbour or his brother,*
> > *saying, 'Know the Lord,'*
> *because they will all know Me,*
> > *from the least of them to the greatest.*
> *12For I will forgive their iniquities*
> > *and will remember their sins no more."*

> *13By speaking of a new covenant, He has made the first one obsolete; and what is obsolete and aging will soon disappear.*

8:7-8 'God found fault with the people' – not with the Old Covenant; he found fault with the people because their sin rendered his covenant weak and useless. The people constantly and consistently failed to live up to their side of the covenant – to obey all that God had commanded them. By its nature it wasn't anything but glorious, and hence Moses' face shone with glory as he communed with God, the God of love who so wanted a connection with the treasured people that would be all his. There is a degree of mystery here, because God knew that the Old Covenant could never achieve this union of mankind with him, but nevertheless the Old Testament came with glory, and when Moses received it his face was enveloped with the glory of the Lord himself. The issue was that the people were at fault. The degeneration from Moses onwards to the point of Malachi is awful enough to tell us that the Law was only there to be a tutor to show mankind that we need a saviour.

Covenant

Throughout the scriptures the idea of covenant is that of a contract with very deep roots in the history of God's people. It is also a solemn and binding promise between two parties: it is serious, it is not to be broken, and it is absolute. There are two kinds of covenant found in the scriptures: one is a contract between two equal parties, who make an agreement together and so form a covenant that has a stipulation. An example of this is marriage, the one covenant on earth that the Lord still requires. Another example is that of Jonathan and David – theirs was a covenant of great vulnerability: they took all their armour off and they agreed to be bonded as brothers and always to be there for one another (1 Sam 18:1-4). A further example can be found in 1 Kings 5:12 where Solomon made a covenant with Hiram, king of Tyre, which included a trading agreement. These covenants between two equal partners often have the word 'brothers' attached to them because they imply some kind of accord or close relationship. There are also some examples of bad covenants made, such as the one Joshua made with the Gibeonites who claimed to be foreigners but in fact were near neighbours (Josh 9).

Secondly, there is a completely different kind of covenant, known as a suzerain covenant, between one who is the Lord and those he is Lord over, with whom he offers to make a covenant. This does not come about by settling an agreement between them, but is entirely on the basis of the Lord's decrees within that covenant. It is an offer made of a covenant of relationship with God, but entirely on his terms and not negotiated. 'When we were enemies of God, we were reconciled to Him' (Rom 5:10). The Lord makes a covenant with humanity, a solemn binding promise that invites us into that covenant, but entirely on his terms. Of course the terms are glorious, but they are his terms. We don't negotiate with God; it is an unconditional, fixed offer. The approach comes from God, they are not equal terms, there is no bargaining. 'He who did not spare His own Son but gave Him up for us all, how will He not also, along with Him, freely give us all things?' (Rom 8:32). That is a suzerain covenant, and an absolutely extraordinary one.

8:8-9 When we look at the Old Covenant, God graciously approached Israel through the angels and through Moses, and invited Israel to come into relationship with him: 'I am offering you this covenant, and here are the ten commandments and all the other laws, which are the terms on which this covenant is going to be based and which you cannot negotiate.' Thus the Old Covenant was a suzerain covenant: the Lord laid out the terms, and of course the people said 'yes' and they agreed, 'All that the Lord has spoken we will do' (Exod 24:3, 7). However, they did not remain faithful to the covenant. If ever a statement has been made which was not borne out by subsequent events, this was it – they never fulfilled their side of the bargain!

8:10   This statement of the new covenant that comes from Jeremiah 31:31-24 is amazing. There is going to come a complete uniting of Israel and Judah so that there will be no more question as to who is included and who is excluded. This new covenant is also a personal invitation from the Lord, no longer just a corporate one. And there are a number of statements of 'I will' – it is God that does all this, he has chosen to intervene and act for his people in these ways.

The first promise is that he will inscribe his ways deep in our hearts, so that we will live according to his law established in our hearts; it will never be an external law again, which we can fall short of and break. This is more than just writing God's commands on our hearts, as for the Old Covenant: 'These words I am commanding you today are to be upon your hearts. And you shall teach them diligently to your children and speak of them when you sit in your house and when you walk along the road, when you lie down and when you get up' (Deut 6:6-7).

God is promising here that he will come and graciously write everything of his ways deep inside us; it was written on tablets of stone in the Old Covenant; now in the New Covenant he gives us a radical new heart: 'I will give you a new heart and put a new spirit within you; I will remove your heart of stone and give you a heart of flesh.' He then writes his ways in our new heart: 'I will put My Spirit within you and cause you to walk in My statutes and to carefully observe My ordinances' (Ezek 36:26-27). This was always God's promise, from the time of Exodus onwards: 'I will take you as My own people, and I will be your God' (Exod 6:7), but now this promise is written deep into the core of our beings. In the New Covenant, God speaks our identity right into the depth of us, into a place that profoundly hears and takes this truth into our beings. We deeply need this affirmation of our relationship with him.

8:11 The second promise can be seen as the ultimate prize that has been won for us in the New Covenant: 'they will all know me.' This goes far beyond the knowing or not knowing of the Old Covenant: 'After that whole generation had also been gathered to their fathers, another generation rose up, who did not know the Lord or the works He had done for Israel' (Judg 2:10). Now there are no graduations of knowing him: all, everyone, will have an ongoing continuous experience of his closeness that only gets deeper and develops even more. The 'all' is so radical. We may have a remnant of belief where we think some people are greater, or we wonder about the least, and who are the least, but God says that now the sacrifice of the blood of Jesus is present there in heaven, *all* will have confident and free access to him, *all* will have an intimate knowledge of him, *all* will be invited to be very close to him, and there will no longer be any graduations left: that was all wiped clean in the New Covenant.

The writer to the Hebrews is saying that all this, prophesied by Jeremiah, has now been made available to us, through what Jesus has done. Father's promise is so radical: 'I'm going to give you a new covenant, I'm going to give you a new heart, I'm going to write my ways in you, I'm going to love you, I'm going to be God to you, and there will be no differences depending on your tribe or race, for all, all will know me now, from now onwards.'

8:12-13 The third promise is just as great: 'For I will forgive their iniquities and will remember their sins no more.' What a promise! Perhaps we will never get to the bottom of the wonder of this, that he will remember our sins no more. There is mystery in this – how does the all-knowing God forget something? How does the God who is outside of time not see things that are in our past? Yet somehow this is the promise that is given us; all we can do is wonder at it. Again, this goes beyond what was given in the Old Covenant, where God had revealed himself to be 'The Lord, the Lord God, is compassionate and gracious, slow to anger, abounding in loving devotion and faithfulness, maintaining loving devotion to a thousand generations, forgiving iniquity, transgression, and sin' (Exod 34:6-7).

So this is the new covenant promise, which takes the idea of covenant far deeper than had been possible before, and reveals more of who this God of ours is. It is a solemn and binding promise from God's side, which says that if we give ourselves to him, if we will surrender all and come with him, his promise to us is that all of these things will become ours. There is absolutely no question; God tells us that he is making a covenant, a solemn binding promise, and never again need those things trouble us. His Son has already paid the price, so that we can have everything.

In the letter to the Romans, Paul grasps the completeness of it: 'He who did not spare His own Son but gave Him up for us all, how will He not also, along with Him, freely give us all things?' (Rom 8:32). Such 'all things' make the New Covenant very attractive. Our shame-based hearts often regulate how much we allow ourselves to receive, how we measure it, who gets what, who is closer, who is in and who is out. We have a horrible measuring line that is all to do with performance, and whether we have earned it or are worthy of it. God tells us to stop all this! He has given us a new heart, he has written his laws within us, he has loved us back to life, he has cleansed us, he will remember our sins no more, and he has declared that from now on all will know him, from the least to the greatest – and that includes us. Whenever we diminish this wonderful covenant that God has offered us, we offend against the blood of Jesus in his sacrifice. When we don't accept that the 'all things' are for us because we are telling God he does not understand how sinful we are, or how undeserving we are, we are not allowing the power of Jesus' blood to attain for us the covenant that he has made.

When we go to a wedding we get a glimpse of God's heart for covenant, which goes far beyond a treaty or agreement. The God of covenant is present at a wedding, and he is speaking there to every human being: 'Do you not understand, this is a window into my heart? Do you not understand, all that is mine is yours? Do you not understand, I will never leave you? Do you not understand, I will never have an eye for another one, my eye is on you because you are the one I love?' That is why a wedding can make us a bit emotional, because we are touching on the God of the covenant, who is opening a window for us.

118

He is telling us to watch the wedding, but to look through that window at his heart behind the event: 'I am the God of covenant, and I will never, ever break what I have agreed to be for you. I will be your God.' In the marriage covenant, the intimate knowing of husband and wife is a window into the depth to which God knows us and wants us to know him; the invitation and the gift of the New Covenant is the answer to the deepest longing and cry of the human heart – to know God and to be known by him. Now our sin has been fully dealt with by Jesus, he remembers our sin no more, and all can truly, deeply, freely, and honestly know him, and be known by him.

Prayer

Father, we are unspeakably grateful for this new covenant that you have offered us through the sacrifice of your Son Jesus. We ask that you would continue to pour your love into our hearts by your Holy Spirit so that we will desire your ways more and more, and that we will grow in intimate knowledge of you each day. Thank you for your promises that you will always love us, that you give us everything we need, that you are our Father God and we are your sons and daughters. We pray this in the name of Jesus. Amen.

Questions

What is the practical difference between the Old Covenant laws being written on people's hearts, and the New Covenant promises being written deeply within our hearts?

When you became a Christian, how was the gospel presented to you? Does the new covenant described here differ from that in any way?

Hebrews 9

Comparisons between the old and the new priesthood

As we saw in chapter 1, the book of Hebrews has been called 'the book of better things,' but there is another title for it: it has also been called 'the book of crossing over' – the root of the Hebrew word for 'Hebrews' literally means 'to cross over' (which hints at the very identity of this people being tied up with their escape from Egypt through the Red Sea and into the promised land). This title captures the overall theme of the book as an invitation to the whole of humanity to cross over from an external system of empty religious behaviour (as it ended up) into something so extraordinarily radical it will take all our days to understand the length and breadth of what Christ has won for us. The crossing over is a phrase relating to salvation, but it also seems that in running our marathon we are often invited to leave behind one season and cross over into something new, because that previous season is ageing and has completed its time. As we continue our journey through this book, the invitation to cross over into something we have not yet inherited is always in front of us.

Chapter 9 of the book of Hebrews is an ongoing confirmation of the wonder of Jesus' high priesthood compared to the Aaronic one. It covers a number of themes that we have begun to look at already, comparing the obsolete and ageing Old Covenant, which is external, and the New Covenant which is totally internal, deep inside our hearts, where a revolution takes place that transfers us from being after Adam to being after Christ. The New Covenant was backed by an oath, it is permanent, and it is all-sufficient. The chapter also describes some details of the earthly worship and sacrifices in the tabernacle, and how these foreshadow the heavenly realities that they point to.

Many of us might wonder why the writer of Hebrews would spend so much time on these things if they didn't have vital significance for our journey of faith. So we have to trust that there are riches in this section to be mined, which we can only touch on briefly, but every word has something important for us. In Hebrews the comparison of new with old often highlights the power of the new and the obsolescence of the old; when we perceive the new we realise just how old the old is, and how powerful the new is that God has given to us. Now through the New Covenant we are absolutely in Christ, for ever and ever for all eternity we are in him; we have been separated from the line of Adam, now we are in Christ.

Chapter 9:1-10

¹Now the first covenant had regulations for worship and also an earthly sanctuary. ²A tabernacle was prepared. In its first room were the lampstand, the table, and the consecrated bread. This was called the Holy Place. ³Behind the second curtain was a room called the Most Holy Place, ⁴containing the golden altar of incense and the gold-covered ark of the covenant. Inside the ark were the gold jar of manna, Aaron's staff that had budded, and the stone tablets of the covenant. ⁵Above the ark were the cherubim of glory, overshadowing the mercy seat. But we cannot discuss these things in detail now.

⁶When everything had been prepared in this way, the priests entered regularly into the first room to perform their sacred duties. ⁷But only the high priest entered the second room, and then only once a year, and never without blood, which he offered for himself and for the sins the people had committed in ignorance.

⁸By this arrangement the Holy Spirit was showing that the way into the Most Holy Place had not yet been disclosed as long as the first tabernacle was still standing. ⁹It is an illustration for the present time, because the gifts and sacrifices being offered were unable to cleanse the conscience of the worshipper. ¹⁰They consist only in food and drink and special washings—external regulations imposed until the time of reform.

9:1-5 The description of the tabernacle is taken from Exodus 25-31 and 35-40 and portrays the earthly sanctuary where Aaron and his sons ministered as a copy or shadow of the heavenly realities. All the elements described were important for the function of the tabernacle, and highly symbolic, yet they had significant limitations in what they could actually achieve for sinful mankind. The lampstand, the consecrated bread, the tables, the altar and the ark are prophetically very important, but they had limits in themselves. Even so, we 'cannot discuss these things in detail now,' much as we might have wanted the writer to have done so; the idea is that all these things no longer have significance when compared to the heavenly realities that they point to.

9:6-10 On the annual day of atonement, the high priest took the blood of bulls and goats on the designated day to cover his and the people's sins committed in ignorance. This was not for intentional sins, but only for covering sins of ignorance. The Holy Spirit highlights this huge limitation of the Aaronic priesthood's role, that none of the offerings could clear the conscience of the worshipper. Under the Old Covenant there is no direct access to God, because our conscience is a barrier, and the blood of bulls and goats is useless in purifying our conscience. Our conscience is our inner awareness of how our conduct, or our intentions, or our character line up with God's ways or requirements. A man's body might be ceremonially clean, but his conscience is still torn apart inside.

Our conscience is like a plumb-line, so where our conduct or intentions don't line up with God's ways, we feel bad, or blameworthy, or actually ashamed, and we long and cry out for a clear conscience so that we can have a close relationship with the Lord. Therefore, in the Old Testament the external was ceremonially cleaned, but the conscience was not cleansed, and without a clean conscience our ability and confidence to approach God for closeness is undermined. This is a profound difference between the two covenants. One is external, the other goes to the very core of our beings, to clean us for intimacy.

Chapter 9:11-15

11But when Christ came as high priest of the good things that have come, He went through the greater and more perfect tabernacle that is not made by hands and is not of this creation. 12He did not enter by the blood of goats and calves, but He entered the Most Holy Place once for all by His own blood, thus securing eternal redemption.

13For if the blood of goats and bulls and the ashes of a heifer sprinkled on those who are ceremonially unclean sanctify them so that their bodies are clean, 14how much more will the blood of Christ, who through the eternal Spirit offered Himself unblemished to God, purify our consciences from works of death, so that we may serve the living God!

15Therefore Christ is the mediator of a new covenant, so that those who are called may receive the promised eternal inheritance, now that He has died to redeem them from the transgressions committed under the first covenant.

9:11-12 Jesus passed through the visible heavens into the blazing centre of the unseen heavenly tabernacle. It is not part of the visible creation we live in all the time, but it is still substance. Just because something is unseen, it doesn't mean that it is not substance; it is just that we need different eyes to see it. Jesus entered having shed his own human blood, not with the blood of bulls and goats. And his blood is the evidence of our eternal reconciliation. Imagine all in heaven, the angels and cherubs, erupting in praise as Christ enters, having shed the blood of his own sacrifice, and sits down at the right hand of the Father, with his blood covering all who want to come back into intimacy.

9:13-14 This is central, and highlights the comparison – 'how much more' – between the effect of the blood in the Old Covenant and the effect of the blood in the New Covenant. The Old Covenant cleansed externally as God intended it to do. The blood of Christ is altogether different: he as the sacrifice was unblemished from his conception to his death, and he offered himself as God's dearly beloved Son, with the result that we get a truly cleansed conscience. We are reconciled to our Father, with a permanent friendship that we never need doubt again, because of the power of Jesus' blood.

How much more indeed! We should be alert that this is the point where temptation sometimes wants to invade us, to try to undermine that absolute confidence that now our consciences are clear.

9:15 This sums up the gains of Christ standing in our place, which covers all previous sins and gives eternal life. A ransom is the price to be paid to break open the doors of a slave's existence, to take them out of that prison and bring them into the glory of true sonship or daughterhood. The ransom paid is the blood-price necessary for every one of us to come into that inheritance. That blood even reaches back to those in the Old Testament who were responsive to God's call. That is incredible: the mercy and love of God reach in every direction to rescue any of us from all the sin and shame that rob us of life and a relationship with our Father.

Chapter 9:16-22

16In the case of a will, it is necessary to establish the death of the one who made it, 17because a will does not take effect until the one who made it has died; it cannot be executed while he is still alive.

18That is why even the first covenant was not put into effect without blood. 19For when Moses had proclaimed every commandment of the law to all the people, he took the blood of calves and goats, along with water, scarlet wool, and hyssop, and sprinkled the scroll and all the people, 20saying, "This is the blood of the covenant, which God has commanded you to keep."

21In the same way, he sprinkled with blood the tabernacle and all the vessels used in worship. 22According to the law, in fact, nearly everything must be purified with blood, and without the shedding of blood there is no forgiveness.

9:16-22 We can imagine this vast covering of blood across everything to do with mankind's dealings with God, because without the shedding of blood, there is no forgiveness. This is God's response to man's sin, to our wilfulness and idolatry and turning away; there is no other way for it to be dealt with but by the merciful forgiveness of God. The shedding of blood does not signify God punishing sin in any way; it is a sign of the covenant of forgiveness.

The writer uses the analogy of a will to help us understand the connection between a covenant and the blood that is shed: the same Greek word *diatheke* is used for both will and covenant. No will can come into effect without the death of the testator that then releases it; just so, the Old Covenant needed death to release or seal it. The blood signifies that if either party breaks the covenant, that is what will happen to them: their blood will be shed. That is the profound nature of covenant. In a reference to Exodus 24:3-8, the earthly things that were sprinkled with blood by Moses included the book of the law, the tabernacle and all the vessels – all copies of the heavenly things – and the people. Moses sprinkled the blood over all of it so that it was ready for the Old Covenant to come into operation, to seal the covenant that God had given him for the people.

Thus the Old Covenant was inaugurated; the people knew how they were to live in order to remain in relationship with God. And the key outcome, which of course we all crave for, is forgiveness, the means of reconciliation and staying in relationship with God. Without the shedding of blood there is no way to forgiveness, but with the shedding of blood, forgiveness is released – in the Old Covenant for external sins, in the New Covenant for every single thing we've ever, ever done. Forgiveness cleanses us and restores relationship.

Chapter 9:23-28

23So it was necessary for the copies of the heavenly things to be purified with these sacrifices, but the heavenly things themselves with better sacrifices than these. 24For Christ did not enter a man-made copy of the true sanctuary, but He entered heaven itself, now to appear on our behalf in the presence of God.

25Nor did He enter heaven to offer Himself again and again, as the high priest enters the Most Holy Place every year with blood that is not his own. 26Otherwise, Christ would have had to suffer repeatedly since the foundation of the world. But now He has appeared once for all at the end of the ages to do away with sin by the sacrifice of Himself.

27Just as man is appointed to die once, and after that to face judgment, 28so also Christ was offered once to bear the sins of many; and He will appear a second time, not to bear sin, but to bring salvation to those who eagerly await Him.

9:23-24 This is the ultimate high priest of all high priests: in the fullness of the New Covenant, Jesus shed his blood and then entered before his Father in heaven, declaring that the sacrifice has been made. He comes before the Father and appears for every one of us for ever more, and the Father's complete approval is enough to validate this covenant. Thus, 'It is finished' continues to be shouted everywhere, in all the courts of heaven, for any man or woman who puts their trust in that blood. It is done, it is completed, and now our access is permanent.

9:25-28 Our identity is not one of sinners saved by grace; our identity is one of cleansed sons or daughters who give great delight to our Father. Sin, the power of sin, has been dealt with once for all. This does not mean that we don't sin, it does not mean we don't fall short, but we are no longer under the mastery of sin that tries to hold us in patterns of sin. That power has been broken and so we are free from being enslaved to sin; sin is done away with. This is a powerful thing. The effect of that sacrifice carries us through to his appearing a second time as we eagerly await his coming.

This magnificent promise is not only that it has been done once for all, never having to be done again, but it means that we can look forward to the time when he comes again, when there will be the utter fulfillment of the initial salvation we have received. We get to receive the fulfillment of that salvation when he comes again, and so we eagerly await his coming back, because we will become like him. Surely, belief in the second coming pulsated in the veins of all believers in the early church, who eagerly awaited Jesus' return. I believe God is bringing back that deep-seated cry in the hearts of many of his children in our time, who are beginning to feel the prayer arising in them: 'Come Lord Jesus, we eagerly await your second coming, when those who followed you will receive the guaranteed inheritance of the fullness of sonship and daughterhood we have been journeying toward.'

Prayer

Father, we thank you that your great desire for us is that we might know you as our loving Father, to be close to you, and experience intimate friendship with you. Thank you for sending your Son to die for us, that by his blood shed on the cross our consciences are fully cleansed from all sin and shame, and we can truly enter that precious relationship that you created us for and have called us into. Amen.

Questions

Is this the season for a 'crossing over' of some sort in your life, to take hold of more of your inheritance as a son or daughter of God? What might that look like?

Is there a burning in your heart for the fulfillment of who you are in Christ, for the completion of your identity as a son or daughter fashioned after the likeness of Jesus? How can you best pray for Jesus to come again, so that you and all around you will be transformed and reach their glorious purpose?

Hebrews 10

Confidence to draw near, full of faith

Some parts of the letter to the Hebrews are not easy to understand intellectually, while others can be quite challenging to us personally at the level of our hearts. In working our way through this letter, there could also be a danger that we focus on certain themes which we are passionate about and forget there are whole other aspects of who God is. If we neglect them, it means we can no longer represent him accurately. In the frailties of our own hearts, we may love certain truths so much that we could end up creating another idol, rather than reverentially expressing well who he is in his entirety. We can create an idol by concentrating on something so much it now becomes who we are making God to be, because it is who we want him to be rather than who he really is.

There is thus a tension between truly representing the more difficult or challenging aspects of who God is, alongside the easy and acceptable face of this amazing affectionate Father that perhaps we have begun to come to know in our personal experience. We want to represent him well, not with our own particular favourite themes, nor out of our past experiences and fears: our past can influence how we think of God, so we need to be aware that our fears and our emotional wounds can also create theology. These need to be surrendered to the word of God, which will create his truth in our hearts of what he is really like. If true revelation about who God is has sunk deep within us and anchored our hearts, then it is not going to be shaken by looking at more difficult themes; he adds understanding as we go along the way.

In looking at the more challenging passages, we should avoid falling into such thinking that God is out to get us, or just wants to punish us, for example, rather than seeing that we may receive revelation here which helps us in our journey. It actually makes us a better son or daughter than we have ever been, because now we understand even more of what he is really like. We can ask the Father to help us to represent him the very best we can, because we yielded to everything he wanted to show us about himself, and he made us more faithful witnesses. As his image-bearers, we want to be faithful witnesses to what he is like, not to please people by presenting him in a certain way. It is easy to please people by presenting God in a way that we know they would like to hear, but it is not always giving the whole picture. Let us then acknowledge the tensions that come along, and not be afraid of the more difficult or challenging issues that arise in our journey through this letter.

Chapter 10:1-10

1For the law is only a shadow of the good things to come, not the realities themselves. It can never, by the same sacrifices offered year after year, make perfect those who draw near to worship. 2If it could, would not the offerings have ceased? For the worshippers would have been cleansed once for all, and would no longer have felt the guilt of their sins.

3Instead, those sacrifices are an annual reminder of sins, 4because it is impossible for the blood of bulls and goats to take away sins. 5Therefore, when Christ came into the world, He said:

> *"Sacrifice and offering You did not desire,*
> *but a body You prepared for me.*
> *6In burnt offerings and sin offerings*
> *You took no delight.*
> *7Then I said, 'Here I am, it is written about Me in the scroll:*
> *I have come to do Your will, O God.'"*

8In the passage above He says, "Sacrifices and offerings, burnt offerings and sin offerings You did not desire, nor did You delight in them" (although they are offered according to the law). 9Then He adds, "Here I am, I have come to do Your will." He takes away the first to establish

130

the second. ¹⁰And by that will, we have been sanctified through the sacrifice of the body of Jesus Christ once for all.

We are coming towards the end of the major section in Hebrews that describes the work of Christ. We have been looking at a number of themes, of high priesthood, the covenants, the blood, the Old Testament, the New Testament, and we are reaching the conclusion of the ongoing argument that the writer of the letter has been presenting: how the death of Jesus has brought about true forgiveness of sins, which the sacrifices and the temple and the priesthood of the Old Covenant pointed to, but could never fully achieve.

10:1 A shadow does not have substance, it is just a lack of something, a silhouette, it is a vague projection of something but it is not the substance itself. 'The law is only a shadow of the good things to come, not the realities themselves.' The good things to come are of course what we have been looking at in the previous chapters: a restored intimate relationship with God, wonderful forgiveness, and being made whole. Those are the realities that the blood of Jesus brought for us, but which the law and all that came with it could never achieve. The law foreshadows these and points towards them as a sign of the real thing, but it could never 'make perfect those who draw near to worship' – which is the goal of Hebrews: to allow ourselves to be increasingly transformed into the likeness of Jesus so that we reach the fulfillment of who we are created to be as sons and daughters of the Father. In comparison to the wonder of the realities, the law has no substance at all.

10:2-4 If the sacrifices prescribed by the law had had any effect on our wilful and internal sins then there would not have been any need for them to be repeated year after year. But of course they had no effect at all, and in fact they were never intended to do so; the blood of animals was only ever designed to deal with the unintentional or ceremonial sins of the Old Covenant, and this sacrifice had to be repeated over and over again – the writer may have in mind here the annual sacrifices of the Day of Atonement (Lev 16). These sacrifices could only point towards the one effective sacrifice of Jesus, which is the only true remedy for the guilt we feel over our past sins. A clear conscience is a wonderful gift, especially when we look back at our past history and there are certain low points of failure, sin, or bad choices, which would still bring a cry of 'oh no,' if we didn't understand the blood of Jesus – even though we know we have been forgiven. It is these 'oh no' episodes particularly, that the blood absolutely cleanses our conscience from and removes all guilt or condemnation. His blood allows us to be completely free from any sense that they have anything to do with our future life.

Some believers are aware that they have done really bad things, things that they would never want displayed on a big screen for all the world to see. In fact, probably all of us have had moments when we look back and think 'oh no, what was I doing, what foolishness, what path did I choose then?' The joy of the blood of Jesus isn't just the knowledge that he has forgiven us, but that our whole conscience, our inner knowledge, the inmost part of our being feels completely clean, and it never needs to be mentioned again, because we have confessed it and repented. That applies to lesser things as well as to terrible crimes or serious sin, which the blood of Jesus is all-sufficient to cleanse completely and forever, so that our conscience is clean. We do not ever have to feel that there is a shadow dogging us, because although we did do whatever it was, the blood of Jesus has come and utterly cleansed us of the sin and the guilt.

10:5-8 God was not saying to the people 'I don't want sacrifices and offerings; I don't know why you are doing all this.' No, he commanded them to be made in the law. What he is saying is that he was not pleased with the outcome of the sacrificial system, because the offerings had become so much the high point of religious duty that the people's hearts were drawn away from true obedience to the One they were worshipping. In this quotation from Psalm 40:6-8, David is not speaking about himself, but prophetically speaking about the arrival of the Messiah, one who comes in the body that has been given to him. This Messiah does not carry out all the ritual of the Old Covenant sacrifices, but he simply says, 'Here I am, I have come to do Your will.'

This follows a theme that runs through the Old Testament which says that once sacrifices and offerings have become merely an empty religious ritual, and do not involve obedience at the level of the heart, they take away the relationship in which God wants us to be all his, and he to be all ours. For example, in 1 Samuel 15:10-35 we read of Saul going to fight the Amalekites, and the Lord told him to kill everybody and everything. When he returned – and this was a low point of Saul's downfall – he had instead captured and brought back Agag, and kept a lot of sheep and cattle to offer as a sacrifice. He was pleased with himself, but he had acquiesced with a looser interpretation or a lesser level of what God had told him. Samuel the prophet arrived and knew immediately that this was deeply grievous to God; he challenged Saul, 'what have you done?'

It is a shocking story; we can imagine Samuel feeling the very grief of God, that the man whom God promoted from nothing to be king had now reached the point where he was appeasing all sorts of things, in himself and others, rather than obeying what the Lord actually said. Saul kept making excuses, blaming his men, and absolving himself of the responsibility of the true calling upon a king of Israel, which was to be under divine authority, to reflect the order of heaven and not be a king for themselves, independent of God.

In another example, God spoke through Isaiah to the people of Sodom and Gomorrah: 'What is your multitude of sacrifices to me?...Bring your worthless offerings no more...I cannot endure iniquity in a solemn assembly...even though you multiply your prayers, I will not listen' (Isa 1:11-15). In Hosea the prophet speaks a similar word from God: 'For I desire mercy, not sacrifice, and the knowledge of God rather than burnt offerings' (Hos 6:6). We can hear the heart of God in these examples: the original sacrifices were God-ordained and were part of the process of keeping the Israelite nation connected to him, but they became more and more a religious duty which the people carried out, forsaking God himself. God is imploring them, 'Today, if you hear His voice, do not harden your hearts' (Psa 95:7-8). In the end, a wholehearted obedience was the kind of sacrifice that God was really looking for; the sacrificial system of the Old Covenant was pointing to a better way.

10:9 Here, Psalm 40 prophetically points to Jesus, who comes to change the whole system: 'Here I am – it is written about me – I have come to do your will.' In the process 'he takes away the first to establish the second' – the crossing over. For Jesus, doing the will of the Father was the hallmark of his life on earth, from his earliest years being 'about my Father's business' (Luke 2:49), through his ministry doing 'nothing by Himself, unless He sees the Father doing it' (John 5:19), and culminating in his submission in Gethsemane 'not what I will, but what You will' (Mark 14:36), and to his obedience 'to death – even death on a cross' (Phil 2:8). Jesus' sacrifice was in utter obedience to the will of his Father; he came to do the will of God.

If we are honest with ourselves, we may identify times in our journey of our trying to please people, which have hindered us from fully obeying God's instruction to us. We may have had times of doing what seemed the right thing to do in others' eyes, rather than listening to God and acknowledging 'You really are my Lord Jesus, here I am to do what you want, and I'm willing to do it whatever anybody thinks.' We might identify the society-pleasing, the fear of what others think, which is what we saw in Saul: costly decisions we have made because we were under the pressure of what people felt, rather than our certainty about what Jesus was saying to us. This is not about independence, it is about the fact that God is far more interested in our response to what he says and our obedience to his will, than in carrying out duties – offering sacrifices – that we think matter to him.

10:10 We have been made holy through Jesus' sacrifice, once for all. 'But now he has reconciled you by Christ's physical body through death to present you holy, unblemished, and blameless in his presence' (Col 1:22). We are blameless, without accusation; the 'accuser of our brothers' (Rev 12:10) has no ground to stand on any longer. Once the blood of Jesus covers our whole being, no enemy in hell can ever point to us and remind us of a dark spot of sin back there in our past. It is finished, we are blameless and free from every accusation.

Chapter 10:11-18

11Day after day every priest stands to minister and to offer again and again the same sacrifices, which can never take away sins. 12But when this priest had offered for all time one sacrifice for sins, He sat down at the right hand of God. 13Since that time, He waits for His enemies to be made a footstool for His feet, **14***because by a single offering He has made perfect for all time those who are being sanctified.*

15*The Holy Spirit also testifies to us about this. First He says:*

> **16***"This is the covenant I will make with them*
> *after those days, declares the Lord.*
> *I will put My laws in their hearts*
> *and inscribe them on their minds."*

17*Then He adds:*

> *"Their sins and lawless acts*
> *I will remember no more."*

18*And where these have been forgiven, an offering for sin is no longer needed.*

10:11-13 'Every priest stands' because they haven't ever been able to finish the job of offering sacrifices, hence they must keep standing. But when Jesus had completed his once-for-all sacrifice, he sat down at the right hand of God. 'After He had provided purification for sins, He sat down at the right hand of the Majesty on high' (Heb 1:3) – he is a king-priest. The sitting down means the work has been done, it is complete, there is nothing more that needs to be added or repeated; there is a tremendous assurance for us in this. No further actions, by us, by priests or anyone else, are required for our sins to be taken away. There is one, single, unrepeatable historical event which was the only sacrifice needed to deal with sin, all sin; we can meditate on it, we can proclaim it, we can remember it, but we can never add to it or repeat it.

Now 'He waits for His enemies to be made a footstool,' till all his enemies are under his feet. Moreover, this is not a passive waiting but a progressive advance of his reign over his enemies: 'Of the increase of His government and peace there will be no end' (Isa 9:7). For example, currently in this nation there is much turbulence, but we must not fall into a political mindset, rather we can simply say 'Come, king Jesus, loose what you want in the middle of this turbulence.' We cannot afford to become political at a time when his kingship is about to increase in the nations. More enemies will be coming under his footstool than ever, because it is a daily increase of his government, his rule and authority. There is nothing static about the kingdom of God, it is forever advancing. Whatever seems to be occurring naturally at the moment, heaven is actively brooding over this nation, reaching into our country, and the rule and reign of our king Jesus is increasing day by day. There will come a time when 'He has put all His enemies under His feet' (1 Cor 15:25), and we will be there to see it!

10:14   The declaration of how God sees us is that we are completely set apart, free from all accusation, blameless in his sight: he has declared it, and now we are in the process of sanctification so that every part of our being becomes aligned with that declaration. We can see clearly what he has said about us, and we can also see the process he takes us on to gain the fullness of what he has declared. The 'being made holy' is guaranteed, if we follow him all our days. Our *position* is settled, complete, we are justified. With regard to the *process*, however, we now walk through the journey to the end point, where as soon as we see him face to face, we will become like him. Justification is foundational, upon which we build the doctrine of sanctification. If we ever put sanctification as the basis, we would all think we are hopeless cases and we will never make it to the end; if we lose the certainty of our position in him as justified, blameless, without accusation, then the process of sanctification is quite disheartening at times, because we are too aware of our failures and forget what the blood of Jesus' sacrifice has actually already positioned us to be.

When I married my wife Sue, I had known her for five months, and we made an astonishingly reckless covenant: 'I will love you always, all that is mine is yours, I will love you with all my heart.' It was all true, but I didn't really know her. We were married, through a marriage covenant in which we promised we would never leave each other, yet it was only then that we began to get to know one another, and the two started to become one. On our wedding day, we made a covenant that 'we will be one' from today onwards, but the journey to become one was a process where God had to deal with our hearts, because there was so much that had to be changed in order to achieve the fullness of what we had actually declared in our covenant on the day. We were married, we were one, but we had to journey deeper into that unity in an ongoing process. It is so important that in the process of sanctification we never lose the underpinning certainty that we have already been declared justified in heaven.

10:15-18 This major section on the work of Christ concludes with a repeat of Jeremiah's prophetic promise, emphasising that, unlike in the old order, Christ's sacrifice is complete and never to be repeated. In the New Covenant, there is no remembering of our sins – where they have been forgiven, no further sacrifice is needed.

Sanctification

The process of sanctification is actually a beautiful one and should never be a heavy, gut-wrenching struggle. 'For those God foreknew, He also predestined to be conformed to the image of His Son, so that He would be the firstborn among many brothers' (Rom 8:29). God knew each one of us before the creation of the world (Eph 1:4), and he predestined us to be conformed to the likeness of Jesus more and more, tomorrow more than today, until our last day when we meet Jesus and we become completely conformed to his image – that Jesus might be the firstborn among many brothers and sisters. Jesus is the firstborn son in a human frame, a perfect son, with perfect trust, in perfect relationship with the Father, demonstrating what true sonship really looks like, and then he invites us: 'I'm the trailblazer, now will you come along behind me, and will you learn how to be just like me, more and more, until you are conformed to my likeness?'

That is the process of sanctification. It is not just that we are a bit soiled inside and we need some help getting clean – although we do. It is not even that we have some roots of sin and iniquity deeply embedded in our hearts that need digging up and removing – we do. But the beauty of the process of sanctification is that God is saying to us each day: 'will you let me change everything about you a little bit more, to become the son or daughter I've longed for and predestined you to be, because that is why my Son died for you.'

Being made holy means being set apart for God. When we gave ourselves to him, our old life was over: 'aren't you aware that all of us who were baptised into Christ Jesus were baptised into his death? We therefore were buried with Him through baptism into death' (Rom 6:3-4). There is a death at that point, we gave ourselves totally, we are all yours, Jesus. It is as though he says to us, 'my blood now declares that you are clean in my sight, you are blameless, you are perfect; now let us begin the journey where I lead you to become transformed into my likeness, to become like me.' Thus the process follows the covenant. Then the more we become sons and daughters after the likeness of the Son, the more we can help bring his reign on earth, and the enemies start to come under our feet. Jesus is the firstborn, he is a son first of all but he is also a king, and he is the trailblazer for us to follow, so as he crowns us with glory on earth, we also bring his enemies under our feet.

Sanctification is about far more than being good and avoiding sin. We can limit our understanding if we think perfect just means sinless, and holy only means doing the right thing. Instead, perfect means complete, and that we have reached our full destiny. Sanctification is not just about getting the bad roots out, but actually about this wonderful conforming to true sonship and daughterhood that he predestined for us before we were ever born, that we would become what we were created for.

Chapter 10:19-25

19Therefore, brothers, since we have confidence to enter the Most Holy Place by the blood of Jesus, 20by the new and living way opened for us through the curtain of His body, 21and since we have a great priest over the house of God, 22let us draw near with a sincere heart in full assurance of faith, having our hearts sprinkled to cleanse us from a guilty conscience and our bodies washed with pure water.

23Let us hold resolutely to the hope we profess, for He who promised is faithful. 24And let us consider how to spur one another on to love and good deeds. ²⁵*Let us not neglect meeting together, as some have made a habit, but let us encourage one another, and all the more as you see the Day approaching.*

With this passage we enter the last major section of Hebrews. We have heard about the person of Christ, and about his profound lasting work through the shedding of his blood on the cross, and the crossing over from the finished old covenant into the new. Now we are going to read about what all this would mean in living out today as best we can the truths that we have discovered. How does all this work in our lives? How do I live in the light of these truths? Theology is great, truths are great, but they need to reach into our daily lives in order to make a difference, to help us in running our race.

We are destined to live ever more fully as the most beautiful sons and daughters that our Father has called. And we should remember that the whole earth and everything in every corner of creation is groaning for us to be revealed as sons and daughters, along with the multitudes of others in every nation who have set their hearts to follow Jesus (Rom 8:19). There is an almost palpable groaning for sons and daughters to be revealed. By every step of obedience we take – 'here I am Lord, I'm here to do your will' – we promote sonship and daughterhood on the earth, because the Father says 'thank you that you are willing to say Yes.'

It may be worth from time to time asking ourselves the question, 'have I obeyed everything he has asked me to do, up to this point?' This is not to be intense or gloomy, it is just a simple question which allows us to keep clear from any drifting away or any empty religiousness that might have crept in. We might also want to pray the most dangerously exciting prayer: 'here I am Lord, send me.' It does not mean we are striving for things to do, but it means we permit him to position us where he wants us to be at this time, for the very best expression that we can give of him on earth.

10:19-21 Addressing us again as brothers and sisters, the writer sums up the essence of the previous major section: we can now all have confidence to enter the most holy place, because the blood of Jesus has been offered in sacrifice once and for all. There is a new and living way into the presence of the Most High God, with a high priest having led the way and now continually interceding for us before the throne of God. This new way is 'through the curtain'. The curtain itself in the temple was 10 metres high, and is said by some to have been about 8-10 centimetres thick. It is speculated that it could not even have been torn apart by two large horses pulling in opposite directions. It took the hand of the Father to tear the curtain from top to bottom (Matt 27:51), which signified that the real curtain, Jesus' body, was rent in two on the cross, his blood shed in order to allow us to enter this place that we absolutely and increasingly want to be in, but which we did not have access to before. His body was tortured, broken, so that the new and living way is opened up for us to go right through.

10:22 Let us draw near to God: this is the great invitation, in the light of all that we have understood so far, which goes out to every one of us, 'will you now come through into that close place with me – I'm inviting you to come with freedom and confidence.' Access is no longer limited to certain appointed people at specific times, who have satisfied all the right conditions. When we look at our own lives, we might find that our confidence and freedom are sometimes subdued because of how we perceive we have been living our lives. We are measuring our freedom by how we are living rather than by the power of the blood of Jesus. We are judging our qualification to enter right into the Father's arms by how well we are living, rather than by the power of the blood of Jesus.

However, the encouragement is 'since we have confidence to enter, and since we have a great priest, let us draw near.' Inside each one of us is a permanent, portable sanctuary, the inner place where we commune with God, and it is wide open. It is no longer out there but is internal. We do not go to a special building, we do not go to a priest, and we do not bring offerings; that is all over and finished with. God's promise was 'I will give you a new heart, I will write my laws in it.' God's passion to find us and bring us close is so intense that we cannot comprehend it if we are evaluating our life by the criterion of how we are living, rather than by the power of the blood of Jesus. So the qualifications that allow us to draw near with a sincere heart are that we have full assurance of faith, our hearts are sprinkled to cleanse us from a guilty conscience, and our bodies are washed with pure water. This is the final conclusion of all the work of Christ that we have read about, so 'now will you come and draw near?'

What does it mean to have a sincere heart? Sincerity means there are no masks, no pretence is needed, there is no routine, no doing things just to meet expectations, that would in any way inhibit absolute honesty and genuineness. Our heart says, 'Jesus, I'm coming to you, because I want to connect with you and I don't care what anybody else thinks.' We cannot afford to reduce this intimacy to outward actions or what we normally do, and miss out on this sincere drawing near of our hearts. This sincerity simply means that God does not want any deception in his family or in our drawing near. We can imagine his passion for us, 'I so want you close for intimate fellowship – all will know me.' He hates pretence just as we would in our own children, feigning to be nice or kind, but we would feel the deceit. He just wants relationship, with no pretending. So, having a sincere heart means that every time we can, because of the blood of Jesus, we run in to his presence with a passionate desire to meet with him, to be with him and connect with him, and not to fulfill some religious duty that we are so used to doing that we forgot the whole idea was to connect with him. 'Blessed are the pure in heart, for they will see God' (Matt 5:8).

We might find this challenges us at times. For example, during a time of worship when we find a hymn or song difficult to sing because of how we are feeling at that moment, we may be tempted to join in with everybody else because that is 'what we do.' We should rather feel free to step back from singing something like, 'Here I am, wholly available' if this doesn't reflect how we really feel; otherwise this would be an insincere following of a routine, rather than a genuine vulnerability that says 'this is where I'm at Lord, I don't think I can sing that today, I think I'll just sit quietly and hope that you can capture my heart again as I give myself to you.' The issue is that our Father does not want the pretence that develops any empty religious behaviour again, rather than having groups of his children come to him eagerly and say 'we won't follow a routine, we'll pursue the way that Jesus has opened up so that we can have that closeness with you.' The encouragement is that in the light of all that Jesus has done for us, we can come with utter sincerity and assurance that this is the offer he made. We can be assured of the portable sanctuary inside us where we can meet with him whenever we want. By Jesus' suffering, he will justify many (see Isa 53:11). We can draw near to God because now we believe, our hearts and conscience have been cleansed by the blood of Jesus, and our bodies are washed in water – meaning we have been baptised, and are united with Jesus.

10:23 Because of the work of Jesus, we can draw near, and we can hold unswervingly to the hope we profess, for he who promised it is faithful. We have heard of the anchor attached to our hearts going in through the curtain and being completely connected to Jesus who is holding us (6:19), so we can hold on unswervingly to the hope – the hope of our destiny, our calling, the promised land, the inheritance we now have, the hope of glory, the hope of his presence living within us (see Col 1:27).

We also hold to the hope that God will restore us to the fullness of sonship, in leading many sons and daughters to glory. The hope in our hearts is not just 'I hope I make it through.' No, it is a confident and favourable expectation that he is wholly committed to finishing the good work he started in us, so that he gets a son or a daughter who is fully his as a son or daughter. Being led to glory is a restoration, a returning to what he always wanted us to be; this is the hope of glory.

There is another hope – the ultimate hope – which is to live with him forever. There is the hope of our life on this present earth, but the more glorious hope is that he is coming back and we will be with him for eternity in a renewed earth, the ultimate hope of all hopes. Without God there is no hope in the world. Therefore, with God all hope is restored, and it is what we were born to have, set deep inside us – whether it is for now, the good coming towards us in this life, or the final hope of eternal life with him.

The unswerving nature of our hope is all part of this marathon, in which we encounter things that buffet and hit us, but somehow the anchor is so firmly fixed, that we do not get swept away by the storm because of something that happened. We hold on determinedly to the certainty of eternal life with him. Often we are not eternally minded enough, so we get pulled apart by the tension between this transient world, and the eternity of heaven – we get so

142

immersed in life, we forget the glorious future that God has set out for us in Jesus. We need to 'hold resolutely to the hope we profess.'

10:24-25 'Let us consider how to spur one another on' – we have looked at encouragement already in Hebrews 3:13-14 – and 'let us not neglect meeting together, as some have made a habit, but let us encourage one another.' This is all the more important as we see 'the Day' of his return approaching. There is a day when this will happen; the Father has set a day, but we do not know when it is and in fact no one knows it (Matt 24:36). We may get signs, there may be things to see happening on the earth which lead us to wonder how far off the day is, but these should not lead us to a conviction about the timing that he never wanted us to have. There is a day the Father has set, when the King of kings will reappear on the earth, and it will be outstandingly glorious, utterly beyond anything; we can be certain that it is coming. So what do we do in the meantime? We keep encouraging one another, because there should be no lone pilgrims. He created a family because he wanted his children to be filled with heavenly encouragement; when one is drifting a little bit to the side the other says 'Come on, don't forget the journey, don't forget the hope, get back on track again.'

This constant encouragement we can give to one another is so important, especially when we get together, and so we need to guard against things losing value that we have previously found great worth in. Boredom might set in that really has no place in the Christian pilgrimage, and we could react to that by saying 'I'm leaving, I'm tired of church, I can't be bothered with it anymore.' The encouragement of meeting together lies in God's presence being at the heart of it all, which attracts us to want to be with each other and with him; a time that makes our hearts surge with encouragement again, rather than feeling we did our duty but we didn't really participate in it fully with a sincere heart.

The Greek word translated here as 'neglect' – *egkataleipo* – is a strong word that means desert, forsake, or abandon. It is the same word Jesus uses on the cross, 'My God, why have you forsaken Me?' (Matt 27:46). This giving up in meeting together might start with something seemingly small on the inside, a change in attitude in our hearts perhaps, just as the drifting away does, but it ends in a forsaking that is significant. For us taking part in the marathon, God does not want pilgrims to step off the path when there is a difficult crossing-over time; he wants us to persevere in meeting together in order to welcome even more of what is in his heart for us, rather than jump off because things became a little difficult.

So, let us not be on our own, let us gather with those we are meant to gather with, because when we gather God comes in a way that he seldom comes to us when we are on our own. When two or three are gathered, there he manifestly is in a way that all of us will know it is him present in the midst of us, and our hearts will be encouraged. We can also have a great time with God on our own, but it should be both, not one or the other. If we neglect one aspect, the other is negated; if we have both, the fire in our hearts is more likely to burn brightly.

We should want our passion to be stirred more and more as the day of his return draws nearer. Let us not give up meeting together and connecting with others, so that the fire burns more in us as we meet with him, and he somehow blows on the embers, realigning us and keeping us from drifting. Our church families are not perfect, but when we meet together it is a different kind of song that arises than when we are on our own.

Chapter 10:26-31

> *26If we deliberately go on sinning after we have received the knowledge of the truth, no further sacrifice for sins remains, 27but only a fearful expectation of judgment and of raging fire that will consume all adversaries. 28Anyone who rejected the law of Moses died without mercy on the testimony of two or three witnesses. 29How much more severely do you think one deserves to be punished who has trampled on the Son of God, profaned the blood of the covenant that sanctified him, and insulted the Spirit of grace?*

> *30For we know Him who said, "Vengeance is Mine; I will repay," and again, "The Lord will judge His people." 31It is a fearful thing to fall into the hands of the living God.*

10:26-28 Here we reach the final warning, which as before will be followed by an encouragement. The writer reminds his Hebrew readers of two principles in the Old Covenant, with which they would have been very familiar. First, the various sacrifices and offerings dealt with ceremonial and unintentional sin, but 'the person who sins defiantly, whether a native or foreigner, blasphemes the Lord. That person shall be cut off from his people...his guilt remains on him' (Num 15:30-31). There is no answer for deliberate sin. Secondly, 'On the testimony of two or three witnesses a man shall be put to death, but he shall not be executed on the testimony of a lone witness' (Deut 17:6). This looks back to the previous warnings we have seen: greater punishments apply now than for the law of Moses (2:2-3), do not turn away from the living God (3:12), do not fall through disobedience (4:11), for there is no way back for those who publicly renounce their faith (6:4-6).

When we consider this warning for those who 'deliberately go on sinning,' we are looking at wilful sin, based on rebellion and pride. When Lucifer, the most glorious cherub, began to rebel, he was saying to himself: 'I will be like God, I am not happy with where I am in my God-given position under his fathering, I want to go up higher; I want to be like God' (see Isa 14:12-13; Ezek 28:14-17). Following on from this pattern, all sin starts with a refusal to receive who God made us to be, and a desire for something else or to be somebody else. If we deliberately, wilfully sin, we are once again looking at the notion of identity before the working out of it. And for this deliberate, wilful sin 'after we received the knowledge of the truth, no sacrifice for sins is left.'

It is not for us to judge the outcome; it is the Lord who judges. But it is for us to look at this passage and see that there is a line somewhere, that having known him – having tasted the heavenly gift, shared in the Holy Spirit, tasted the goodness of his word and the powers of the age to come – if we then turn away with an absolute intention to blaspheme against God, and we persist in this, then the passage is here to tell us, 'do not think that does not matter in heaven's eventual judgment.' In our time, where grace is seen to be so all-encompassing, we can drift into thinking it no longer matters how we behave, because his grace covers it all, and this can tip into a universalism that says 'surely the God of love wants everybody to be close to him, whoever they are.' It is thus a mistake to think that because God is love, he will not deal with those who deliberately and persistently reject him; but how he does that is up to him.

This raises many questions: what kind of judgment is coming, if it is the Lord who avenges? Is God's grace effective for all, or not? What about hell, because that does not sound consistent with a God of love? These are important issues that require consideration, discussion, and answers from hearts that are open to God's truth.

10:29-31 For those who have entered into the New Covenant and said 'Yes' to God, but then stepped out of it again and stamped on it, saying 'No,' they are behaving in a shocking way against the blood of the Son of God. This is doing something blasphemous, counting as rubbish the precious blood that Jesus Christ shed for us, to make a new and living way before the Father. Hence, while it is not for us to judge others, there is something there that acts as another caution for ourselves, 'do not even go near the sign: cliffs – erosion.' Do not even approach the sign, because that is the beginning where something starts inside us and it grows to become wilful and deliberate. Then we start to think 'I don't care, I don't think you are that important, God, in fact I'm not even sure you exist'. This leads easily into thoughts of, 'We don't need a God, I'm going to champion the wonder of human beings who will make it without God.' So although we once knew him and have gone through that new and living way, now we have moved out of it again and are treading on the very blood that made that way, which enabled us to draw near to him.

It is God's place to judge, not ours. The writer quotes from Deuteronomy to make the point, 'Vengeance is Mine; I will repay...For the Lord will judge His people' (Deut 32:35-36). The measure of judgment is commensurate to the measure of revelation, and this is addressed to those who have received 'the knowledge of the truth.' Jesus had a harsh warning for some of the unrepentant cities in which he had worked miracles: 'Woe to you, Chorazin! Woe to you, Bethsaida! For if the miracles that were performed in you had been performed in Tyre and Sidon, they would have repented long ago in sackcloth and ashes' (Matt 11:21). God promised: 'All will know me,' all will have an intimate and progressive relationship with me, and so if they have had that and then they turn away, there is trouble there. If they have not encountered that kind of relationship, if they have circled around some of these things but they have never yet come through the door, then we do not know so much about God's judgment on them. There is a line which can be crossed, but it is not for us to say when this has happened.

We can wonder how it is possible for somebody to turn away from God, if they had really known him. How could someone be disobedient to what they know to be true? It must be to do with the measure of revelation in their heart. However, we are never, ever called to make any kind of judgment about another person on these matters, we are just called to look at that event and tremble a bit considering our own marathon and think 'Lord, by your grace, please keep me, all the way to the finish, and never let me even begin to deny what is so precious that you have given me.' We can never know how or why this might happen in others, but many of us know people in our journey whom we have grieved over, because they did know God but have then turned right away. We still cannot judge them. All we can understand is this: deep emotional wounds are often the doorway to the beginnings of an inner reaction that turns against God; the pain they cause reveals that there is a process of healing that needs to be gone through, without which the wounds will cause more and more harm. We will see more about that a little later on.

Whatever happens to us in our journey, we always have a choice at every step of the way. We are never robbed of our choice by things that occur in the journey, even by the way our fathers and mothers can affect our view of God. We can never blame those things as a reason why we go off the road: we always have a choice. Otherwise, we feel we are victims and the power of the blood of Jesus isn't enough because of what happened to us. God wants to root out of us any victim sentimentality, or self-pity, which just clouds the wonder of our one run in the race, with our Father alongside us every step of the way. In the book of Kings, despite having the most terrible father kings, some sons came along who led great revivals. Conversely there were wonderful kings whose sons went completely off course and led their people into idol worship. Families, upbringing and circumstances are important, but we still have a choice. Lucifer too had a choice.

God insists, right through the heavenly realm and the earthly realm, that every single being has a choice, because he wants voluntary lovers. God is love; he has surrounded the whole of his unseen and seen realm with a deep longing that the love he has for his creatures will be reciprocated, and so there will be the greatest song ever. Therefore, there is always choice, which is why we pray for those who have been struck down in the journey, that they would be lifted up again and receive the spirit of grace, because he is always willing to give the necessary empowering grace for us to get up and run again.

That is the warning and now there is an encouragement to follow. This is all about a call to keep going on our marathon journey with God.

Chapter 10:32-39

32Remember the early days that you were in the light, when you endured a great conflict in the face of suffering. 33Sometimes you were publicly exposed to ridicule and persecution; at other times you were partners with those who were so treated. 34You sympathised with those in prison and joyfully accepted the confiscation of your property, knowing that you yourselves had a better and permanent possession.

35So do not throw away your confidence; it holds a great reward. 36You need to persevere, so that after you have done the will of God, you will receive what He has promised. 37For,

"In just a little while,
He who is coming will come and will not delay.
38But My righteous one
will live by faith;
and if he shrinks back,
I will take no pleasure in him."

39But we are not of those who shrink back and are destroyed, but of those who have faith and preserve their souls.

10:32-34   Not many of us in the West have been publicly exposed to insult and persecution because of our faith, but around the world today there is more persecution of Christians than at any other time in the past. The letter to the Hebrews therefore very much speaks to our current age. In fact, we may well soon find ourselves standing side by side with those who are being insulted and intimidated, discriminated against and persecuted. But how was it that the Hebrews could accept the confiscation of their property 'joyfully'? We are entering a section in the letter where the Lord will be calling us more and more to look at the ultimate prize, so the perspective we get on our current struggles is governed by the joy of what is absolutely promised at the end. In Hebrews 11, the chapter on faith, we will encounter this viewpoint that if we can glimpse what is ahead of us, it will greatly affect our capacity to handle what is happening now, even if that is very turbulent.

The writer is saying here in chapter 10, 'Remember' – the Hebrews seem to have been in a better place in the past than they were now, because in their earlier days they were experiencing much persecution, and yet they were so convinced of their heavenly reward they were able to rejoice in the midst of it. Perhaps we are already seeing more persecution in my own nation, the UK, right now. Evidence is available of the increasing number of anti-Christian episodes happening in the country over the last few years. When we hear testimony of faithfulness and joy in such situations, and know that perhaps we will be next, it helps us to remember how to stay at rest and be able to handle some outburst against us because of our faith, and so we build up our own testimony which encourages us further.

10:35-39 Persevering with what we have been given to do guarantees a rich reward, a closer intimacy with God, a deeper joy, a greater trust in his provision. We do not hear a lot of sermons on rewards, probably out of a concern that they will turn into talks on performance. But we need to understand rewards from a true biblical standpoint, because there is something God has provided in a reward that gives us a huge source of encouragement to keep going. There is a difference. As soon as we turn rewards into a performance game we lose the whole point of them. But we are going to be richly rewarded, and we need to persevere so that when we have done the will of God we will receive what he has promised, 'for, in just a little while, He who is coming will come and will not delay.' So this is not just for the end: it is in our journey that we wait for him to come in some way, when perhaps we begin to lose heart or we begin to drift a bit, and it is as though the writer is saying, 'no, no, keep going, so that when you have completed what he gave you to do, you will see the fulfillment.'

This quotation from Habakkuk 2:3-4 leads us towards the examples of faith in the next chapter. But what about those who shrink back, 'I will take no pleasure in him' (v 38)? Perhaps we are stepping out boldly in what God wants us to be and do, then some things happen which are intimidating or undermining, and we begin to think: 'I'm going to withdraw a bit, I'm going to step back because I don't like the awful pain that this situation is causing, and I don't think I've got what it takes after all.' We are not giving up or leaving, but we are starting to shrink back. One of the lies of the enemy is that we do not have what it takes, making us question if it was really God leading us. One example of this occurs with Nehemiah: Sanballat opposed Nehemiah rebuilding the wall in Jerusalem. He attacked Nehemiah's surety and confidence by undermining him continuously in an insidious, attritional way, sending people up who spoke intimidating comments to the people building the wall: 'What are these feeble Jews doing?...Can they bring these burnt stones back to life from the mounds of rubble?' (Neh 4:2). Nehemiah prayed that God would 'turn their scorn back upon their own heads' (Neh 4:4) and continued rebuilding the wall. This is a prophetic pointer to how the enemy tries to undermine us and cause us to shrink back from the fullness of what we were given to do.

Persecution is widespread across the earth, and although we may not be suffering directly ourselves, we are probably aware that in times of persecution a radical flame is lit in many hearts that leads them to really become true followers of Jesus. There is no compromise in that atmosphere. And so the writer to the Hebrews encourages us to say, 'if these things are happening, if there is persecution, let us not be the ones who shrink back because things have become difficult, or because we are undermined or intimidated or we are just tired.'

I was in a situation recently that caused me to shrink back from the sharp end of what I believe I had been given to do. I began to shrink back because of a painful misunderstanding, which set off all sorts of chain reactions, and internally I felt, 'I don't want to do this anymore, I don't like this challenging work.' But then there was a whisper inside me that said, 'you are really not fit for this game, are you? You don't have it.' I started to look at other people and I thought, 'they've got it, I'm probably the wrong person.' It took a few weeks to sort out the pain inside that had made me shrink back like this. The most challenging aspects of what we are called to are where we will experience the most battering, because that is where God causes us to bring a new invasion of his kingdom into our situation. We can think it does not matter if we don't do the little bit we are called to do, that somebody else can do it. But it does matter: this is our calling, we have no idea what God will do through these seemingly small areas of obedience, even if there is a cost attached to it. When we mess up in life, or miss opportunities, it can often centre around abdicating from what God has given us to do in crucial moments, because of the pressure or the pain that it was causing us.

We need to be aware of all these elements that surround and affect our journey, so that we are a bit more alert to what the enemy likes to do. Then we can pray for confidence to fill us. This is the surety that our Father in heaven is saying 'I believe you have what it takes, I believe in you.' The marathon we are running is a partnership, not a lone run. We are partners with the Father who owns the whole universe, and we do not have to struggle along thinking 'Here I am running, and I hope he's with me.' Let us not shrink back and get destroyed, but push on in faith and be saved.

Prayer

Jesus, we thank you for the hope that you give us, the hope of our calling, the hope that you will lead us into the glory of the fullness of sonship and daughterhood, the hope that we will live with you for ever. We acknowledge that at times this hope becomes dimmed in our eyes; please restore and strengthen our hope so that it never ceases to shine into the successes and struggles of our daily lives, that we live always in the light of that glorious future with you. Amen.

Questions

Have there been times when it was difficult for you to say, 'Here I am, God, I have come to do your will'? Have you obeyed everything God has asked you to do, or have other things subdued or appeased the call to live as one of his sons and daughters?

Do you have confidence to enter the Most Holy Place and draw near to God with a sincere heart? What might limit that confidence? What can you do to spur one another on in such faith and confidence?

Hebrews 11

Inspired by those who ran before us

For many years I had a 'geographical' view of heaven and earth, based on all sorts of misconceptions, I believe, but the basic one was Jesus 'ascending' in Acts 1, going upwards, giving the impression that heaven is somehow a fair distance 'up' from the earth. There was also a kind of false religiosity in my thinking that contributed to this idea that heaven is far up above us. That view of things is really damaging, because deep inside it gives us the feeling that we have to pass through quite a distance upwards to get anywhere near God. I believe a more correct view is that heaven and earth are interweaved in a horizontal plane, perhaps as two intersecting circles, with a thinness where they are very close, or where one is overlapping on the other. The actual meaning of 'upwards' then is not the same biblically as though we are going 'up' to the third or fourth floor, but rather it has a different meaning altogether.

If we think of this intersection of heaven and earth engaging with each other, we may more easily become aware of heavenly beings in the room with us right now, such as angels, or a cloud of witnesses. They are not far away in a tiny balcony way up beyond the atmosphere. The word 'up' has to do with priority and superiority, not a geographical position. So when we are in God's presence, perhaps encountering him there with us, we can somehow sense heaven in the room, because the veil has moved aside, and heaven is invading our earthly space without us having to try hard to welcome heaven in. One of the adjustments the book of Hebrews invites us to make is to be more aware of, or more comfortable in, the unseen realm than in the seen realm, because that is our real home, that is where we really belong.

The writer now leads us into a sort of hall of fame of the heroes of faith, of which there are many including the biblical characters, but also famous Christians who have walked the earth over the centuries, and our own set of heroes in our lifetime who we have looked at and gained huge inspiration from. God planned for all of those to be there to encourage us when it is our turn for the marathon. They contribute to our race, with testimony, with joyful examples, challenging words, but all the time whether biblically, historically, or now in our day, they add to our sense of energy and passion to run the journey well.

We are each called to our own unique race that is marked out for us, and in this we can experience the pleasure of God, when we are right in the mainstream of what he made us for. When Eric Liddell, the missionary to China, was competing in the Olympics, he had to contend both with religious pressure to do what seemed right by not running on a Sunday, and the world's pressure to fit in and participate on their terms. But he remained assured in what he had to do; he knew where heaven's pleasure was. Each of us needs to pioneer our own race to get into the slipstream of where Father's pleasure is, because that is the only thing we can do on earth that gives him glory. Avoiding any religious 'ought to' or the world's mould is part of the navigation in our race.

When we experience the pleasure of God in running our unique race, something inside us knows deeply that this is what we were born for: we feel fruitful, it is easy, it is not a heavy yoke, there is no pressure on us and we feel as though we have come alive. Part of our prayer in the marathon, therefore, is for the Holy Spirit to keep nudging us right into the centre of the race marked out for us, because then we will bring him the greatest glory by going on *that* race, and not another. Sometimes people can pressurise us into doing or being something that although we were born for it, it isn't the right time yet. We need to be asking, 'When Lord? Where? How? What is the timing?' Our lives will then be adding to the next generation's run, just as previous generations' lives are encouraging us in our own race. Both now, and when we have gone on to glory, our lives will continue speaking something to somebody, somewhere, that will make them think, 'if you did that, I'm encouraged to do this, because your life inspired me.' There is a sort of passing of the baton in our marathon races in this way.

Chapter 11:1-7

¹Now faith is the assurance of what we hope for and the certainty of what we do not see. ²This is why the ancients were commended.

³By faith we understand that the universe was formed at God's command, so that what is seen was not made out of what was visible.

⁴By faith Abel offered God a better sacrifice than Cain did. By faith he was commended as righteous when God gave approval to his gifts. And by faith he still speaks, even though he is dead.

⁵By faith Enoch was taken up so that he did not see death: "He could not be found, because God had taken him away." For before he was taken, he was commended as one who pleased God.

⁶And without faith it is impossible to please God, because anyone who approaches Him must believe that He exists and that He rewards those who earnestly seek Him.

⁷By faith Noah, when warned about things not yet seen, in godly fear built an ark to save his family. By faith he condemned the world and became heir of the righteousness that comes by faith.

11.1 Faith is being sure, being convinced. It is like holding a title deed to something in our hand, which ensures we are going to get the goods we have the right to. Faith is being sure of what we hope for, and certain of the whole life we have been called to. Faith is not something we reach out to get hold of; on the contrary, we are born to have faith, we are each righteous ones and therefore we already have faith. Faith is being sure of what we hope for, and certain of what we do not see. So, for all the heroes of faith, God has spoken to them and this word has caused them to see something in their spirit or in their imagination, and what they see hasn't been seen yet, but they are convinced it is going to happen. It is a lifetime of living like that. As Paul wrote to the Corinthians, 'we fix our eyes not on what is seen, but on what is unseen. For what is seen is temporary, but what is unseen is eternal' (2 Cor 4:18). We are not talking about faith that leads to salvation; this is about promises and about the end – living out a marathon of faith. 'I have been crucified with Christ, and I no longer live,' – it is the end of me as a natural person. I no longer live, I don't exist as I was – 'but Christ lives in me. The life I live in the body, I live by faith in the Son of God, who loved me' (Gal 2:20). Overall, the whole journey is one in faith; when I ended my old life in baptism, I began a life of faith.

11:2-3 The first example the writer gives us is that once upon a time there was nothing, just a void, emptiness, it was not there. It was not as if God had a lot of material and said, 'let me see what I can do with this, because I'm quite creative.' No, there was nothing, and he said, 'Let there be light,' and there was light (Gen 1:3). So something came into being that hadn't been there simply because the Creator spoke it, and when he says something, it has to happen. The writer is offering us an example of faith. Whatever our position on how science and reason fit in to explain the sequence of events in creation, the writer is pointing to a matter of faith here. God is saying, 'will you trust me? There was nothing, I spoke, therefore it came into being: what a wonder.' By faith we believe that at one point there was nothing, God spoke, and it came into being, he made something out of nothing. And here is the point: faith is not making a big effort to bring our minds to believe something unbelievable; faith is always in an actual person. It is the person who does it that convinces us that the event is going to happen.

11:4 Cain offered some of his crops, and Abel offered a sacrifice from his livestock, the fat portion of the firstborn of his flock. God looked with favour on Abel's sacrifice, but on Cain's offering he did not look with favour (Gen 4:3-5). How did Abel know that the favour had come and how did Cain know that the favour had not come? Abel had made his offering by faith, 'this is what the Lord wants and I'm going to do what he wants, with the sacrifice of the best.' Perhaps something in Cain's attitude was bringing his sacrifice more as a religious duty, thinking 'I'll bring some of my crops as an offering.' Somehow the Lord did not ask for that. There must have been something not right in Cain's heart, for the Lord told him, 'If you do what is right, will you not be accepted?' (Gen 4:7). The writer of Hebrews tells us that 'by faith Abel offered God a better sacrifice than Cain did.' Abel was a righteous man (Matt 23:35) and therefore a man of faith, but Cain's actions were evil (1 John 3:12), revealing unbelief in his heart. The consequences were profound and awful.

11:5-6 Enoch did not experience death, and before he was taken he was commended as one who pleased God. We learn that without faith – this is a central verse in the chapter – it is impossible to please God: 'If he shrinks back, I will take no pleasure in him' (10:38). No wonder the disciples said, 'Lord increase our faith' (Luke 17:5). Enoch walked faithfully with God for 300 years, as an early pre-patriarchal figure, and then one day he went to be with the Lord. There was something in Enoch's life that demonstrated faith in the Lord, which spoke, 'I want to walk with you and be faithful to you.' The Lord must have been so pleased with him, that in the end he went directly to be with the Lord.

Faith

It is really interesting that while Jesus was on the earth, even he as our king sometimes seemed surprised at certain people's faith. He was amazed at the centurion, 'I am a man under authority, I understand what that is like and when I say to men go, they go; will you just say the word?' (see Matt 8:8-9). The centurion did not even feel he was worthy to have Jesus come under his roof, so worthiness wasn't the issue – although we want it – but nevertheless he still asked Jesus just to say the word, and it would happen. That sort of faith seems to draw God's attention more powerfully than anything else; it seems to draw him when we dare to say, 'Lord just say the word,' or 'I will just touch the hem of his garment' (see Matt 9:21). Another example of great faith is the Syro-Phoenician woman, who just would not let go of Jesus, saying, 'let the dogs eat the crumbs, I want what you have, I will not let go of you Jesus; I believe you have it for me, and my faith is now being sure of what I hope for. I'm certain about you' (see Mark 7:25-30). This was not an entitlement issue – she just believed in what she hoped for, and it was irresistible to Jesus. He is absolutely thrilled when we launch out in faith towards him over something. It gives God such pleasure as a Father, just as any father would have when his children go out on a limb and trust him.

'Faith comes by hearing' (Rom 10:17). God is the initiator of faith – we cannot conjure it up by ourselves, but he sends his word and we respond to it. It all begins with him, and it is our response to that word which pleases him. There was a moment when something changed inside me towards God, where I was overwhelmed both with how good he is, seeing his affectionate face towards me, and with how great he is, which was like hearing him say, 'I can do anything if you trust me.' I don't believe we can trust somebody we do not know, and so our journey in the marathon is actually one where we increasingly get experiences of just how much he loves to move on our behalf if we dare to trust him, and every experience builds up a bank of trust where we are moving from faith to faith – we are built up from faith into ever greater faith. The biblical characters were very honest, 'Lord, help me, I believe, help my unbelief' (see Mark 9:24). They were in that journey of ever-increasing faith, and similarly, the response we make seems to allow us to graduate to another level of trust. Indeed, today if you hear his voice, do not harden your hearts, but believe and trust. Next year our faith will be stronger than this year, because we respond to him and say, 'yes Lord, I will follow you, I will be obedient to you in that as well.'

11:7 Noah's faith and trust in God was remarkable. He lived in an arid, land-locked area, where perhaps the people had rarely ever seen rain. The Lord said 'I've had enough of the violence on the earth and the corruption of man's heart, and I'm going to destroy it all. Noah, build an ark' (see Gen 6:13-14). What was it in Noah's heart that found enough faith, that ability to obey and to build the ark just like the Lord had told him, despite being in such an arid place, and then to fill it with animals and persevere though there was still no sign of rain, suffering the mocking and jeering of men all around him? Somehow God gave him the faith to believe that what God had foretold would in fact happen. The people laughed at him while he trusted that the word of the Lord would come to pass, and then the rain fell.

Chapter 11:8-19

8By faith Abraham, when called to go to a place he would later receive as his inheritance, obeyed and went, without knowing where he was going. 9By faith he dwelt in the promised land as a stranger in a foreign country. He lived in tents, as did Isaac and Jacob, who were heirs with him of the same promise. 10For he was looking forward to the city with foundations, whose architect and builder is God.

11By faith Sarah, even though she was barren and beyond the proper age, was enabled to conceive a child, because she considered Him faithful who had promised. 12And so from one man, and he as good as dead, came descendants as numerous as the stars in the sky and as countless as the sand on the seashore.

13All these people died in faith, without having received the things they were promised. However, they saw them and welcomed them from afar. And they acknowledged that they were strangers and exiles on the earth.

14Now those who say such things show that they are seeking a country of their own. 15If they had been thinking of the country they had left, they would have had opportunity to return. 16Instead, they were longing for a better country, a heavenly one. Therefore God is not ashamed to be called their God, for He has prepared a city for them.

17By faith Abraham, when he was tested, offered up Isaac on the altar. He who had received the promises was ready to offer his one and only son, 18even though God had said to him, "Through Isaac your offspring will be reckoned." 19Abraham reasoned that God could raise the dead, and in a sense, he did receive Isaac back from death.

11:8 'The God of glory appeared' to Abraham (Acts 7:2), and said 'Leave your country, your kindred, and your father's household, and go to the land I will show you' (Gen 12:1). The God of glory who made something out of nothing, who brought creation into being by the power of his word, now appeared in some visible form before Abraham. Then what was it in Abraham's heart that so radically trusted what God said, not even knowing where he was going? He had been living in a city where idol-worship was widespread, and it was there that the Lord looked for a man who would trust him: 'let me find a man in Ur who worships idols, who has never heard of me, has had nothing to do with me, and I will call him to be the father of many nations' (see Acts 7:2-4, Gen 17:5). What happened in Abraham's heart that enabled him to say: 'Okay Lord, I'll go, I don't know who you are, I don't know where I'm going, but Yes'? There must have been something about that encounter with the God of glory that changed him in a profound way.

Faith is a strange thing. When God speaks to us, it gives us the opportunity really to dare to trust that we can do what he asks, because of who it is that is asking. Abraham's response was amazing: he left his land and his people, not knowing where he was going. He simply obeyed and went. His obedience was the external working out of his inner belief in the one who had spoken to him.

11:9-10 Abraham did not make his home in the promised land, although he believed that promise was going to be fulfilled. God 'gave him no inheritance here, not even a foot of ground' (Acts 7:5); all that he received was the promise. He did not settle down and start to build houses, but he lived in tents because he could not even settle in the promise, because he was looking for a completely different city as the real fulfillment of that promise. How had he seen that city? How had Abraham seen a city that God, as the architect and the builder, was building somewhere in the unseen realm, with the vision of that city even stronger than the promise he had received? Abraham must have had some glimpse of that city, so glorious that it motivated him to keep going in faith, and he could not settle in the land of promise: 'I'm a pilgrim on the move to a final destination that is far more glorious than anything on this earth.' Where is that city? It is us – we are the city of Zion, we are his people, we are the bricks and the buildings, and of course the fulfillment will be the new Jerusalem that comes down out of heaven, prepared as a bride (Rev 21:2), as the ultimate completion of what Abraham saw thousands of years beforehand.

All in all, Abraham, the father of our faith and the friend of God, did not know where he was going, but he did know where his inheritance was. He obeyed and went because he trusted the one who appeared to him. He lived in a place that was not yet his home, living in tents, looking forward to the city built by God, the heavenly Jerusalem. This greater longing was behind the promise and the journey and the temporary home. Often we dream too small (and we strategise too large): pilgrimage is living with a dream and a burning heart for something greater and bigger, while we are living in a home that is not really our final home. Something in us on this marathon needs to be dreaming and burning for the finish line, for our inheritance, our destination, for our final glorious home.

11:11-12 Knowing who the promise-maker is enables us to believe the promise, even if the abstract promise itself is too much to understand. Abraham considered that the one who made the promise was faithful, and that was enough for him to believe even in the face of apparent impossibility in his and Sarah's old age: he was 'fully persuaded that God was able to do what He had promised' (Rom 4:21).

However, we should remember that Abraham did not live a completely righteous life. The record of God of these heroes of faith does not shy away from including people who also failed from time to time. Abraham did seek a son from Hagar when the waiting seemed too long, which does not seem to us to have been God's desire for him. He was a liar as well, and not just small white lies (see Gen 12, 20). In fact, all these men and women of faith are not heroes because they led magnificently holy lives; they are heroes because they dared to persevere in faith despite some of the struggles and issues they encountered in their journey. So every one of us has the qualification to be a hero, not because we have cleaned up our lives completely, but because we have dared to believe God at times when he has spoken. In the Old Testament, God has not left out the failures and sins of his people, although he does not dwell in detail on these either. He tells us 'that is what happened,' but in the end what he records for us here is the comfort that their faith is what he loved about them. Of course, the blood of Jesus stretches back retroactively, so they are all cleansed and forgiven of their sin in the same way that we are.

11:13 What was it that Abraham was promised but did not receive? He did have his son, but he did not see the eternal city, he did not see multitudes of his descendants, and he did not see the land become theirs. He did not see the nation develop when God had said 'I will make you into a great nation' (Gen 12:2). Surely he dreamed of that – if he dreamed of the eventual city, then surely he dreamed of his descendants inheriting their land and living in it. He might have thought, 'Isaac was so long in coming, twenty-five years in fact, so surely if God had fulfilled his promise in the first year I would have begun to see the descendants more quickly?' Abraham must have been looking for the ultimate city and the promises of God, yet he died without seeing them, although he died in faith.

Do we want to take our last breath remaining fully in faith for all we have ever known he wants to do, perhaps not having seen what was promised but being part of the accumulating journey that brings that promise into being? We do not want our old age to be a time when our faith is dwindling away and we are just living out our final years. God never intended old age to be what this world has made it: it is an absolute robbery of the older saints of God who have made their journey and who have made such a difference in the realm of faith, birthing the eventual promises even though they did not see them. We can probably all think of people that we know in the prime of their older age, praying prayers and interceding like Anna (Luke 2:36-37), still looking for the promise to come, and they just don't stop. They keep praying, 'come on Lord Jesus, come on Lord Jesus,' and the sound gets louder, not quieter, as the years go by. Their bodies may be frail but their spirits are so burning in faith. That brings such an intense pleasure to the Father.

11:14-16 Abraham could have gone back to Ur or to Haran, (places of his family origin), but once he had glimpsed something of the unseen, he could never want to return to those places because he was drawn to what could not be seen. We may have dreams for our own lives, our families and our cities, and once we have this picture of something, we cannot leave it alone because it won't fade away. We have to persevere with it, and think, 'Lord even if I'm wrong I would rather believe that, than have things stay as they are at the moment, however impossible it may look.'

If we truly glimpse a dream of what we think is in God's heart, we would rather lean in and believe him for it, remaining in faith for it however long it takes, and so contribute to the birthing of God's ultimate desire for our lives and those around us. We cannot go back, as we have glimpsed a better country. God created us to partner with him in what he is bringing about on earth. If we keep on trusting him in faith, it pleases him deeply, he is proud of us, he is not ashamed to be called our God – even if, like Abraham, we have not lived entirely blameless lives. 'I will be their God, and they will be My people' he declares over us (Jer 31:33).

11:17-19   The offering of Isaac as a sacrifice was such a devastating event for Abraham and stretched his faith to the absolute limits (Gen 22). Even if the things we dream of, that we dare to believe God could do, are seemingly taken away because we have absolutely nothing left that we could look to in order that they might ever come about, we can still believe he could resurrect them from the dead. Even if we have to die to something that seems to be utterly crucial to get there, we can still trust that he will bring about his promise to us. Although God had promised that it would be through Isaac that Abraham would have many descendants, Abraham did not hesitate to obey God's instruction to sacrifice his 'one and only son.' From Abraham's point of view, God raised Isaac from the dead, because Abraham was absolutely ready to use the knife, to sacrifice his son. After all, he is 'the God who gives life to the dead and calls into being what does not yet exist' (Rom 4:17). We can have God's creative faith inside us that can call something that does not yet exist into being.

Chapter 11:20-31

20By faith Isaac blessed Jacob and Esau concerning the future.

21By faith Jacob, when he was dying, blessed each of Joseph's sons and worshipped as he leaned on the top of his staff.

22By faith Joseph, when his end was near, spoke about the exodus of the Israelites and gave instructions about his bones.

23By faith Moses' parents hid him for three months after his birth, because they saw that he was a beautiful child, and they were unafraid of the king's edict.

24By faith Moses, when he was grown, refused to be called the son of Pharaoh's daughter. 25He chose to suffer oppression with God's people rather than to experience the fleeting enjoyment of sin. 26He valued disgrace for Christ above the treasures of Egypt, for he was looking ahead to his reward.

27By faith Moses left Egypt, not fearing the king's anger; he persevered because he saw Him who is invisible. 28By faith he kept the Passover and the sprinkling of blood, so that the destroyer of the firstborn would not touch Israel's own firstborn.

29By faith the people passed through the Red Sea as on dry land; but when the Egyptians tried to follow, they were drowned.

30By faith the walls of Jericho fell, after the people had marched around them for seven days.

31By faith the prostitute Rahab, because she welcomed the spies in peace, did not perish with those who were disobedient.

11:20-22 This passage speaks of the issue of passing the baton to generations after us, and affecting their run in the race by our faith. It is not simply about us achieving our destiny, it is about us fulfilling why God put us here, in a way that our children and our grandchildren are blessed because we walked in faith. So what was Jacob praying for in faith as he blessed each of Joseph's sons (Gen 48)? It was the generational theme: the promise. It was the promise, still waiting there, of a great nation and their own promised land to live in. In these few verses there is a sense of something passing through the generations, and it does not matter whether we have children of our own or not because there is always another generation we can affect by passing the mandate on to them. The promise of the kingdom of heaven coming is still there. We are not only doing our best for our children, but we are blessing their journey so that they go beyond us, and our grandchildren go beyond them, and so the increase continues because we were prepared to bless other generations and not just see what is in it for us.

The staff represented Jacob's life, it was his life companion, which had witnessed with him so much of God's goodness, and so he was leaning on this testimony, this story of his life and of what

God had done. Out of that place he was looking forward to the fulfillment of all the promises in the generations to come. And why did Joseph want his bones taken into the promised land after his death (Gen 50:25)? There was something in Joseph's heart that wanted to be there because he had lived the same hope – the highway to the eternal city ran through his heart and he was on pilgrimage to the same destination.

11:23-29 Moses, like the other heroes pictured here, looked forward to something he could only glimpse by faith. He regarded the disgrace of being treated as a slave alongside his own people as of greater value than all the treasures of Egypt which he had grown up with 'for Christ.' He persevered in leading his people out of Egypt because 'he saw him who is invisible.' Something in Moses understood that there was a bigger story, a bigger future out there for his people, and this dimly understood prospect urged him on in faith and in trust in the one he had glimpsed, in belief that there was something better to be had for those who persevered. He trusted that God would deliver the firstborn of his people from the destroying angel (Exod 12:22-23), and that their pursuers would not destroy them either at the Red Sea (Exod 14:21-28).

11:30-31 The walls of Jericho fell because Joshua believed the word from the Lord, given through an angelic being, and obeyed the instructions (Josh 5:13-6:5). The priests and the army had faith that the city would fall into their hands. Rahab also believed, as it was 'by faith' that Rahab 'did not perish with those who were disobedient.' The Israelite spies came from Joshua to investigate Jericho, and ended up in a prostitute's house (Josh 2:1). Once again not all in these narratives are heroes because their lives are blameless. Something in Rahab began to testify, 'I've heard about your God, I've heard how he defeated all the other nations, I've heard what a magnificent God he is, and our hearts here in Jericho are trembling, so I want to be with your God.'

Why did the writer specifically name a prostitute among the heroes of faith? Because she signifies something very important that God wants us to understand about his deep delight in those who will trust him, even when they are surrounded by the mess of their lives and their personal histories. The spies promised to save her and her family if she tied a scarlet cord in her window, which set her apart for rescue and salvation (Josh 2:18) – the scarlet cord which runs as a theme right through the Old Testament until the blood of Jesus is shed.

In the New Testament, Rahab is held up as an example of faith being made evident by her actions (James 2:25). She is also named as the mother of Boaz, in the line leading to Jesus (Matt 1:5). Somehow God entrusted the lineage of the Son of God to a prostitute – faith brought redemption, she was restored, she became a mother, and Boaz became father to Obed, grandfather of king David, and hence down the line to Jesus. In this same genealogy we also see that Solomon's mother had been 'Uriah's wife' (Matt 1:6). Somehow God wants to remind us of David and Bathsheba as also being in the line that brings God's Son to the earth. It is as if God is saying 'Rahab and Bathsheba are central to the story; I will not have it that it has anything to do with man's ability to be righteous that allows him to be part of this extraordinary eternal promise.' God decrees that it is those who have faith who will be part of the generational line, because they could see something that hadn't yet happened, and they join the ranks of those prepared as a bride in the new Jerusalem. How God loves and honours faith in his people!

Chapter 11:32-40

32And what more shall I say? Time will not allow me to tell of Gideon, Barak, Samson, Jephthah, David, Samuel, and the prophets, 33who through faith conquered kingdoms, administered justice, and gained what was promised; who shut the mouths of lions, 34quenched the raging fire, and escaped the edge of the sword; who gained strength from weakness, became mighty in battle, and put foreign armies to flight.

35Women received back their dead, raised to life again. Others were tortured and refused their release, so that they might gain a better resurrection. 36Still others endured mocking and flogging, and even chains and imprisonment.

37They were stoned, they were sawed in two, they were put to death by the sword. They went around in sheepskins and goatskins, destitute, oppressed, and mistreated. 38The world was not worthy of them. They wandered in deserts and mountains, and hid in caves and holes in the ground.

39These were all commended for their faith, yet they did not receive what was promised. 40God had planned something better for us, so that together with us they would be made perfect.

11:32-38 All these heroes are very human, being used by God in great power despite their significant failings and weaknesses. Gideon made an idol from gold and 'all Israel prostituted themselves by worshipping it there, and it became a snare to Gideon and his household' (Judg 8:27). Barak was reluctant to lead Deborah's army without her going with him, and the honour of killing the enemy commander Sisera fell to Jael instead of him (Judg 4:6-22). Samson's weakness for women led him to give away the secret of his great strength to Delilah (Judg 16:1-22). Jephthah vowed to sacrifice the first thing to come out of his house if he beat the Ammonites in battle, but it was his only child, his daughter who came out to greet him (Judg 11:29-40). It is clearly God who uses these men for his purposes; there is a divine power which routs the enemy and turns weakness into strength, because it has nothing to do with human might or righteousness. The spirit of God came upon Jephthah, and upon Gideon and Samson, and they 'became mighty in battle, and put foreign armies to flight.'

It was Daniel who 'shut the mouths of lions' (see Dan 6:16-23), and Shadrach, Meshach and Abednego who 'quenched the raging fire' (see Dan 3:19-27), all believing in God's power to save them from death, and proving faithful witnesses before Darius and Nebuchadnezzar. The women who 'received back their dead, raised to life again' were the widow of Zarephath for whose son Elijah prayed (1 Kings 17:7-24), and the Shunammite woman whose son Elisha had prophesied and subsequently prayed for (2 Kings 4:8-37). The writer probably had in mind the Maccabean martyrs who 'were tortured and refused their release' (2 Maccabees 7). God grants faith to his people in all sorts of different situations; he uses weak and flawed human beings and invests them with his power for his purposes.

167

There are many people in the world now who are going about their ordinary lives but who at any moment may be forced to choose either to recite verses from the Koran or to have their throats slit. In a moment of time the option is in front of them, and the whole of this chapter seems to be about those who said 'No, I will have my throat slit but I will not deny the Lord Jesus.' Or it might be a choice between denying their Christian faith or being raped: 'No, I cannot deny his name.' So there are heroes of faith living in our times too; it is a huge step to take in the journey where they can give up their lives for the one who saved them. But God invests them with power in their frailty and weakness, because there is something beyond this world, something beyond what can be seen and experienced without faith, something better, something greater which enabled these heroes and can enable us to endure suffering, in the hope of an eternity with Jesus our great high priest. The world was not worthy of them!

11:39-40   None of these heroes received what had been promised. In fact, only when Jesus comes back, and the whole company of believers is joined together – the heroes of faith known and unknown, along with ourselves – will the ultimate promises God made to Abraham finally begin to come to pass. God has better things for all of us, beyond what we can see but which by faith we have each glimpsed something of: a life with Jesus in the presence of the Father in the new heavenly Jerusalem.

Prayer

Father, we thank you for the gift of faith, by which we can see into the unseen and glimpse something of the wonder of living with you as our Father, now and always. Please give us more faith. We thank you for these examples of men and women of faith and for others that we know. May that fire so burn within our own hearts that we would live always trusting in you, never doubting your word to us, believing that you are all we need in every circumstance. We ask this through Jesus your Son. Amen.

Questions

Can you think of heroes of faith that you know or have encountered in your own journey? What is it about their faith that you think particularly pleases God?

What is the basis of your faith in God? How does faith differ from trust?

Hebrews 12

The fruit of deepening sonship

Chapter 12:1-3

¹Therefore, since we are surrounded by such a great cloud of witnesses, let us throw off every encumbrance and the sin that so easily entangles, and let us run with endurance the race set out for us. ²Let us fix our eyes on Jesus, the author and perfecter of our faith, who for the joy set before Him endured the cross, scorning its shame, and sat down at the right hand of the throne of God. ³Consider Him who endured such hostility from sinners, so that you will not grow weary and lose heart.

12:1 Where is this great cloud of witnesses? As we found earlier, it is not on a tiny balcony in heaven thousands of miles above us, but they are all around us. How many witnesses are there? There have to be many, many millions of those who have gone before us, whose hearts have been set on pilgrimage, and now they are part of the great cloud, somewhere in the mystery of the nearness of heaven where we are, and they are indeed with us. There is a joining up of that testimony of theirs with our journeys that is very powerful, and there are two aspects to this: one is that they are witnesses to us of what it is like to make a pilgrimage and get the crown at the end, as they know what that is like, and secondly they are witnesses of our journeys, watching us and encouraging and urging us on in our own race.

Crowds are very encouraging when you are running a race. We can see the difference when a runner is struggling and almost giving up and then the roar of the crowd somehow gives them a second wind. I ran a half marathon a few years ago, and remember thinking at one point I was going to have to stop, when I came round a corner and found a whole group of friends and family gathered, shouting like crazy, and this had the effect of causing me to rise up again and keep going. I thought 'if you are going to make that noise for me, then yes I have got it in me, thank you for reminding me,' whereas before I had felt on my own, thinking I was going to give up. They were shouting my name, 'Go on, Paul, go on,' and I thought: 'Yes, I will, I will, I can do it, I can make that last stretch which just seemed impossible.' The power of witnesses and cheering crowds who have already run their race is a very strong sound in our spirits. We may know others who have died and are now there, in the crowd, perhaps laughing wildly and saying, 'Go on, keep going, you have no idea how significant your race is.'

So therefore, in the light of all the heroes of faith we have just heard about in the previous chapter, since we are surrounded by such a great cloud of witnesses, let us throw off every encumbrance, everything that hinders us. What kind of things are these? The world's attractions, our busyness, the cares of this world, worries and anxieties, what other people say about us, perhaps wounds in our hearts. Sometimes when we go to a gym, we can have an elastic strap tied around our ankles to give us more strengthening exercise for our leg muscles – it is hard work, but after we take it off we find it much easier to run. Or, we can train for a race by running with a backpack on, and then feel much lighter on the day of the race. If something is holding us back, it slows down the pace of the run that God wants us to make, and so we are encouraged here to throw it off, whatever it is. In addition, we clearly also need to throw off anything that is sin, which will so easily entangle or obstruct us, or become an obstacle for us in the race.

Indeed, 'let us run with endurance the race set out for us' is one of the great themes of Hebrews. And the race marked out for us is one that no one else can run; this is not a competition, ever. Orphans compete, but sons and daughters realise they have been given their own race, and it is already marked out as to how it is to go. For each one of us the Lord had marked out a race while we were in our mother's womb, so we don't need to compete. Sometimes we may have strayed off the path, and perhaps we did not even know God for many years. At times we may think we have been knocked off course, but the most important thing is our capacity to get back on the track, and begin running again the race marked out for us. We cannot run someone else's race; we can learn and be inspired by them but we cannot run their race because we are marked by our own. In their training, elite runners are sometimes shown old video clips of previous runners to see how they ran a particular race. Clearly sometimes seeing how other people ran their race can inspire us to run ours, but no one can run our race for us.

If we get knocked off the track, it might take us time to get back on again, but when the Lord does lift us back onto the path, it is usually with a greater speed than we ever had before, and with a greater fulfilling than ever before. In his graciousness he says, 'Come on, I'll teach you what you needed to learn from that knock.' Sometimes we can start to feel insecure and look to others, wondering, 'maybe I should do what you are doing, maybe that is more significant, and I should be doing that?' This pattern of thinking is an utter denial of the race marked out for us by God, which no one else can run. It is marked out because it goes the way God wants it to go, until we appear before him in Zion.

Sometimes we may feel it is a competition rather than a pilgrimage, or sometimes we can think, 'I hope I make it to the end, or maybe somebody else will get the praise instead of me.' The truth is, all who participate get their own 'Well done,' and the winning is not about how well we performed. We win if we did our best to keep on track with God's plans, right to our last breath, so we go out in faith straight into his arms. The 'Well done' will be stunning.

Pilgrimage

Psalm 84:5-7 tells us that those who derive their strength from God, and who have set their hearts on this pilgrimage through life with him, are blessed with a particular blessing from heaven: 'they go from strength to strength.' Then it says, 'As they pass through the Valley of Baca, they make it a place of springs; even the autumn rain covers it with pools' (Psa 84:6).

The valley of Baca is the valley of weeping and tears. When the pilgrims go through the valley of Baca they leave behind testimony as springs of refreshment for others, and then they go onwards from strength to strength until they appear in Zion. This is a little snapshot of the journey that many of us are on, where our hearts are set on pilgrimage because we have glimpsed something too great to let go of.

A pilgrim is different to a traveller, a tourist, a wanderer, or a globetrotter; they are utterly different. Blessed is he whose heart is set on pilgrimage. Some of us in our journey have been through a valley of tears, with a loss or a disappointment or something else that caused a really painful valley part of the journey, but because we have travelled through it as pilgrims rather than as travellers, and we have not made it our home, this leaves springs of living water behind as our testimony, which form a pool that others can drink from when they are going through the valley of Baca. They come and drink, and the rains from heaven fall as though the Lord loves the way we have journeyed and left a pool of refreshing testimony, and as he rains on the pool, this increases the blessing for those who then drink from that pool. Meanwhile, we continue on from strength to strength until we appear in Zion. These seasons of tears are not one-off experiences: we go through difficult periods, but the hearts of those who are set on pilgrimage do understand there are valleys of Baca and there are times of weeping to pass through.

As we go through these times, it is helpful to hold onto Father's hand, where we can grip onto him and learn how to say, 'Abba, Father, I'm still here,' and when we do so at the worst of times, it leaves behind a greater pool than when things are going well. We need to understand in the context of the generations following us that when we leave behind a pool of testimony for people to drink from, they know it was our experience, and not just our theology. This experience enables us to carry on from strength to strength, determining not to stay there and make it our home, because as we will see, staying there creates a place or pool of bitterness, which nobody wants to drink from. Instead, people want to drink from a pool of testimony which the Lord has rained on and grown, because he is so pleased with how we navigated that particular valley.

12:2-3 Let us fix our eyes on Jesus: 'Since you have been raised with Christ, strive for the things above, where Christ is seated at the right hand of God. Set your minds on things above, not on earthly things' (Col 3:1-2). There is a capacity in us by which we can set our hearts, set our minds, and we can fix our gaze – otherwise God's word would not ask us to. We can do it; we genuinely have the capacity to keep the call of the king central to our focus. We have the ability to take off what entangles us and to loose ourselves from sin. Doesn't sin drag us down in our race? Doesn't it entangle us and hold us back? And doesn't the baggage of unforgiveness hold us down when we could be running the race with the pleasure of God all over us?

'Let us fix our eyes on Jesus, the author and perfecter of our faith.' Jesus is the trailblazer or pioneer, but he is also the initiator, the author. When I was born again I thought I had found God and come to him. That was my internal reaction. The truth is, he was the one that had been looking for me, found me, and brought me home. In fact, he started it: he was the author. I cannot say that I decided to follow Jesus – no, he surrounded me with so many things until the moment came when he had corralled me, he had captured me, and said, 'Now I've found you will you come home?' That is a beautiful thing: he is the author and he is also the finisher and the perfecter. We should love that kind of commitment to us from God, that he is absolutely committed to us in our race.

'For the joy set before him' – what was this joy? Throughout his life on earth Jesus delighted in doing his Father's will; he only did what he saw his Father doing (John 5:19), and he sought only the will of the One who sent him (John 5:30). Part of the joy before him was the knowledge that he was obedient even to death, and in this he felt the Father's pleasure, the Father's favour. However, there was also joy in knowing that he was bringing to fulfillment the Father's great purpose, that of reconciling human beings to the Father, of bringing many sons and daughters to glory. God's delight is in seeing his children brought back into relationship with him, through the death of Jesus on the cross and his resurrection to new life, with Jesus the firstborn of many brothers and sisters. What greater joy could there have been in the heart of Jesus going to the cross, than knowing the great plan of salvation and restoration of mankind was about to reach its culmination?

After he endured the cross, he 'sat down at the right hand of the throne of God.' It is all done, it is finished. The words from the cross 'it is finished' (John 19:30) are some of the most profound three words in the whole of the gospels, because they are declaring forever something final, never to be revisited. Then, within a few weeks the King of kings ascended and sat down at the right hand of the Majesty, his work done, completed for ever.

'Consider Him who endured such hostility from sinners, so that you will not grow weary and lose heart.' God wants to refresh us, to strengthen us, because weariness can lead to us losing heart. If we get too weary, we have nothing left with which to pull ourselves back into the running and we lose our heart for the race. In our weariness we can hear these words of encouragement, 'He increases the strength of the weak...those who wait upon the Lord will renew their strength' (Isa 40:29-31). There is a process where the Lord steps in and says, 'I want so much to refresh you, that you will not lose heart,' because he does not want us to lose anything of our desire for the race; it is our heart that has the passion to make the journey through to the end.

What a promise this is! There is something only the Lord can do which invades the weariness and gives our strength back. We saw it in chapter 11 where he turned weakness into strength for those heroes of our faith. This is about the race, persevering, fixating on Jesus, having this heavenly vision and getting rid of everything that gets in the way of the running. Sometimes in a race, the runners fall onto the ground after they pass through the finishing tape; they give everything and then when they cross the line they collapse. What God does not want is for us to fall on the ground before we have reached the tape, never completing the race. However, this is a race of two, we are not on our own, because our Father is our helper, and 'He will never leave you nor forsake you' (Deut 31:6). The Lord is our helper in the race.

The story of Derek Redmond in the 1992 Barcelona Olympics 400 metre race illustrates this well: when he pulled up in the back straight with a hamstring injury it was his father who ran onto the track, pushed away the officials, and eventually helped him over the finish line. Naturally, the crowd was roaring because the real winner of the race was this man who got up from the ground and somehow, with his father's help, kept running to the end. Stories like these are tiny prophetic pointers to the wonder of a heavenly Father who is absolutely committed to finish what he began in us, and to give us strength when we feel weary or unable to continue in the race.

Chapter 12:4-11

4In your struggle against sin, you have not yet resisted to the point of shedding your blood. 5And you have forgotten the exhortation that addresses you as sons:

"My son, do not take lightly the discipline of the Lord,
and do not lose heart when He rebukes you.
6For the Lord disciplines the one He loves,
and He chastises every son He receives."

7Endure suffering as discipline; God is treating you as sons. For what son is not disciplined by his father? 8If you do not experience discipline like everyone else, then you are illegitimate children and not true sons. 9Furthermore, we have all had earthly fathers who disciplined us, and we respected them. Should we not much more submit to the Father of our spirits and live?

10Our fathers disciplined us for a short time as they thought best, but God disciplines us for our good, so that we may share in His holiness. 11No discipline seems enjoyable at the time, but painful. Later on, however, it yields a peaceful harvest of righteousness to those who have been trained by it.

12:4 'In your struggle against sin, you have not yet resisted to the point of shedding your blood.' Here the writer is referring to the early martyrs, who had already given their lives along the way in their race. Although the Hebrews to whom he was writing had not encountered martyrdom in their community, they had known persecution.

12:5-6 This passage about discipline has been profoundly challenging to me personally, because it opened something up for me that honestly changed my perspective of God's true fathering. In the marathon, the race marked out for us, the writer to the Hebrews now describes a really important part of the training to enable us to continue the race right to the end. 'In bringing many sons to glory' – we always need to hold in mind that the goal of the work of Jesus Christ is to lead many sons and daughters into glory (2:10).

The whole issue of the Father's discipline is a big area that I avoided for so long because I just wanted to know that he loved me and was a kind Father who would look after me. These are precious foundational truths we never want to move away from, the wonder of being so deeply loved by a heavenly Dad who believes in us. But I didn't understand the role of discipline in the fathering he has absolutely committed to me; 'I will be a Father to you' (2 Cor 6:18) is a firm promise from the very heart of God. I never quite realised the length and breadth of what that would mean, because although we start with the fact that he absolutely loves and accepts us, there is a problem as soon as somebody mentions the word discipline – all sorts of alarm bells start going off inside us. Discipline brings up the idea of punishment or chastening. We have to handle the subject with care, because believers will get offended if their image of a kind Father who will give them anything they need is shattered when hardship comes along, and he is not the Daddy they thought he was. This passage should be given to young believers at the beginning of their journey, so that they understand the nature of discipline and don't misinterpret it, and become so offended that they give up the journey.

Quoting Proverbs 3:11-12, the writer points to two things that might happen when we are disciplined: either we take it too lightly, and do not realise what the Father wants to do, or it seems too much for us to take and we lose heart. Either are dangers if we do not understand the nature of what God is doing in the hardship: we either think 'no, he wouldn't be like that, he's a kind Daddy to me, I'll sort it out,' and so we minimise what he wanted to do deep inside us with the two-edged sword of his word, or we misunderstand it and it causes us to lose heart. In fact, actually understanding the Father's discipline, and welcoming it when it comes, is a really important part of making the journey to the end. We can be assured that the Lord disciplines those he loves.

12:7-11 The writer goes on to support this statement by appealing to the natural parenting process. What happens when parents do not set any boundaries for their children as they are growing up? The children go wild, and they feel unsafe and insecure, because there is no sense of boundaries being there to enable them to live life to its fullest, as God wanted them to. The boundaries are not limits to stop them being who they are, but they are wise borders which cause them to be the best they could ever be in his pleasure. If children do not have any boundaries when they are growing up, it can actually become frightening for them. Although outwardly they are wild, deep down they have become insecure and even lose the knowledge of who they are. The writer is saying if you do not get disciplined, it is almost as if you are illegitimate, without fathering. It means that you don't belong anywhere, because whoever should have been doing that was not there to do it, and they have left you orphaned from the joy of being held by a truly loving father, given right boundaries, and being disciplined and cared for right through these difficult times. Part of the process of discipline is actually to say 'No'. To hear 'No' said to us when we are growing up is really important because it teaches us that we are not here to get our way, but we are here to give our very best for our Father.

All discipline is painful, and some of the things that happen in our lives are painful. Of course, we are not promised that we would never have any pain. The purpose of discipline is to align our hearts to his, and to change our minds about things which we were ignoring, to bring us to repentance, so that we can have the fruit of repentance which is peace with God. When we do not listen, because our minds are set in a direction which isn't consistent with him, and we have either not seen this, or have been unwilling to see it, he brings it to our attention, so that we can live sanctified in that area of our life and share in the fruit of righteousness. The purpose of discipline is always to bring us to repentance over something where we need to change our mind or behaviour.

When we encounter hardship or lack, we can complain, 'Why don't you give me what I want? You said you would give me everything I needed'. This is a strange misunderstanding of the wonder of what real fathering is about. Each of us has experienced some events that have been really hard to go through on our journey, such as a loss, or a betrayal, or perhaps our money dried up, or a relationship broke down, or a great promise never came to pass that we were sure would come about, or we just felt crushed in some way. If we interpret these hardships as in any way reflecting a change in God's absolute loving commitment to us, we step into the realm of 'he loves me, he loves me not' – we are starting to gauge his love for us based on how things are going on around us, and whether things are how we wanted them to be. We need to get to the point of realising, 'If only I hadn't behaved like I did earlier on, I might have better received his discipline, because his discipline is never punishment.'

If we see discipline as punishment, it means we feel pushed away and associate it with involving some sort of harsh treatment that dismisses the person from the realm of fathering, and sends them out somewhere else, because we have been 'bad.' Punishment involves fear, as we are told, 'perfect love drives out fear, because fear involves punishment' (1 John 4:18). Punishment then introduces a difference in the relationship such that now fear is in there, and we fear we are going to be punished again and again or pushed away, and the whole relationship is altered. Discipline, on the other hand, says, 'Come here, I want to get closer, to create greater sonship in you, and I'm going to have to let some circumstances come around you which will cause you to heed what I'm up to: welcome it, and then you are going to live even more as who I made you to be.'

'Should we not much more submit to the Father of our spirits and live?' We don't like the word 'submit,' but it is in our spirits, our inner beings, where he most wants to be the father we long for, so every time we submit to whatever he is doing in the hardship, we are allowing him to father us at our very core. When we say 'All right, Father, it is painful but I surrender to you,' we receive life, we are more deeply fathered, we become more completely the sons and daughters he created us to be. In these moments we say 'Abba' more profoundly than ever, causing our hearts to love him more fully. The more we pursue this, the more we come into our inheritance. Submitting and allowing our Father truly to father us through circumstances that we find painful, sometimes deeply painful, is actually the way we most profoundly encounter the one thing we long for, and somehow this fathering brings us a step further into our true identity as his sons and daughters.

Submitting is a challenging process as there is a letting go of our own will and trusting in someone else. In submitting, our trust is saying that we really do believe he works everything for our good. It is always painful, but it is written here to help us understand that when it is painful, it does not mean he doesn't love us. When it is painful it does not mean he is subtly punishing us. We have to put that way of thinking aside and say, 'I submit, Father, I don't understand this, but I'm willing to endure the pain so that you can change me, so that I can share in your holiness, your otherness, in who you are as God.' We get to share in that nature because we allow him to discipline us. The calling to be conformed to the likeness of his Son will mean the Father's discipline comes again and again, to cause our hearts to come in line with his best for us. We may misunderstand it in our immaturity and question why he is doing this, but all the time the Father is asking us to let him change us, saying 'I'm not going to force myself, but if you submit, you will live beyond where you have lived before.' We are never to misunderstand it.

There are two other things in his disciplining to watch out for and avoid. One is self-pity, which we know is an awful state of mind: we can catch ourselves moaning, 'it's just not fair, why can't you answer this?' The pressure is on and we can be grumbling with self-pity because it seems too much, 'you don't understand Lord.' The other thing to avoid is a sense of being a victim, having a victim mentality, 'poor old me,' or 'you have no idea how bad it is.' For here is the Father's face, always turned towards us with such a deep affection, saying 'Will you submit, will you come with me in this, because it will transform your journey.'

Chapter 12:12-17

12Therefore strengthen your limp hands and weak knees. 13Make straight paths for your feet, so that the lame may not be debilitated, but rather healed.

14Pursue peace with all men, as well as holiness, without which no one will see the Lord. 15Be careful that no one falls short of the grace of God, so that no root of bitterness will spring up to cause trouble and defile many. 16See to it that no one is sexually immoral, or is godless like Esau, who for a single meal sold his birthright. 17For you know that afterward, when he wanted to inherit the blessing, he was rejected. He could find no ground for repentance, though he sought the blessing with tears.

12:12-13 This section flows on from the previous one as a continuum, so we need to ignore the paragraph breaks which have been added in the translation. If we let it flow as a continuum, the chapter starts with the race marked out for us, it encourages us to fix our eyes on Jesus and keep with him as we run, the author and the finisher, then it moves into the father's discipline, and now it is continuing with issues that get in the way of our race.

'Therefore strengthen your limp hands and weak knees' so that if you are lame with hurts or injuries, you 'may not be debilitated, but rather healed.' The writer is quoting from Isaiah, 'Strengthen the limp hands and steady the feeble knees!' (Isa 35:3), for then will the eyes of the blind be opened, ears unstopped, the lame will leap, and mute tongues will shout for joy. The redeemed will walk on a highway called the Way of Holiness and enter Zion with singing (Isa 35:5-10). There is a great reward for those who continue on the journey, having gathered their strength and courage.

On this race marked out for us there are things that can make us weaker, in one way or another, and the Lord tells us to strengthen those areas, do what you need to do, so that the lameness does not turn into a more permanent disability because you would not process the weakness back into strength again. We know what happens: we can be injured and become lame for a time, but we can seek healing for it so that we are able to run again, or we can become lame but we do not pay attention to it, and then it causes a disability to develop which means we can never run like we were meant to run. The writer is not being harsh, he is saying that in this great race, we should not miss any opportunity to strengthen what has become weakened, to heal what has become lame or injured, so that we do not become incapacitated. We do not want to get into the arena of disability because we have not allowed the Father to take us through some strengthening process in order to get healed. We do not want to miss out on the joy, because we are now in some way disabled.

12:14-17 We are then given four areas that are potential ways in which we can be debilitated or become disabled, so to speak. The first is to 'pursue peace with all men, as well as holiness' – that is the goal, sharing in his holiness, his otherness, so that we will see the Lord. We are to make every effort with all our relationships, each and every relationship, to make sure there are no gaps, there are no unresolved issues, there is no lack of forgiveness, there are no judgments towards those people, there is no offence taken, where we can be subtly playing a game of perfect outward appearances but inwardly avoiding people because we have issues with them. Make every effort and 'If it is possible on your part, live at peace with everyone' (Rom 12:18). It is all too easy when we feel a bit bruised to think, 'a bit of avoidance doesn't do anyone harm, does it?' But that is not the scriptural way.

Jesus tells us 'if you are offering your gift at the altar and there remember that your brother has something against you, leave your gift there before the altar. First go and be reconciled to your brother; then come and offer your gift' (Matt 5:23-24). This seems quite a big initiative to take on our part; if it is their problem, surely they should come and sort it out if they want to? No – if I am worshipping along with a friend and sense there is something between us, I need to stop and come to him and ask, 'Are we OK? Is there anything I've done that has put our relationship out of joint?' God is deeply concerned that all our relationships are actually flowing and connected, there is peace, there is absolute oneness, so that his presence can come upon us more and more strongly.

If there is something not right in my relationship with a friend, I have to act and make every effort. That means it *is* an effort, particularly when we feel a bit bruised and fed up with something. We can feel like Peter asking, 'how many times do I need to forgive? That was so painful what they did – but I forgive them!' (see Matt

18:21). This is something I believe passionately; I see so many gaps and fractures between people. We can take as our goal to 'pursue peace with all men,' so that for anybody who walks through the door from our present lives, or our past history, there is nothing we should have cleared up but have not done so. This is especially important if there happens to be some bread and wine in the room, if we are contemplating celebrating unity within a church family setting. If we like to share bread and wine amongst us, let us first go and be reconciled to our brother or sister.

The second issue that stops us running well is the warning to 'be careful that no one falls short of the grace of God, so that no root of bitterness will spring up to cause trouble and defile many' (12:15). This refers to a warning in Deuteronomy, to make sure no one turns their heart away from God and worships the gods of other nations: 'make sure there is no root among you that bears such poisonous and bitter fruit' (Deut 29:18). What might seem like a small turning away in our heart can take root, and this root can grow to produce a bitterness which is deadly. I have learnt over the years how powerful it is that if we do not resolve issues stretching back in our personal history, or issues that remain today with an individual, and we make judgments towards another, then that starts a negative journey which ends up in bitterness. A root of bitterness is really big trouble, because roots are where we nourish our hearts from, they are where we drink from. That is why Paul prays that we be 'rooted and grounded in love,' in order that we may have power to comprehend how great God's love is (Eph 3:17-18), because our hearts can often instead be rooted and grounded in bitterness, and we drink more from that than we do from his love and his grace.

'Be careful that no one falls short of the grace of God.' If his grace was lifted off our lives today, we would feel its absence very quickly, even though its presence may sometimes be an intangible awareness. If the grace went away, we would know it. We live under the spirit of grace, empowering us, loving us, enabling us. So we must see to it that we don't miss the grace of God, by letting bitterness spring up because we would not deal with the issues deep down that have so pained us, and instead we have judged others. Bitterness defiles many. Is there anybody around us who has been defiled by our bitterness? Bitterness stems from our hearts and seeps into our voices and into our manner, and it contaminates all those around us with this horrible taste that they now imbibe because we are spreading it. It defiles others' journeys because we did not deal with it in ourselves. It is like a poison: it disables us and spoils our race, and it spoils the race for others too.

The third area which can potentially disable us is this: 'See to it that no one is sexually immoral.' The whole cry of the New Testament is for us to 'flee from sexual immorality' (1 Cor 6:18). Why should we flee it? Because it chases us, and its subtle entangling around us means that if we go anywhere near it, it will quickly grab us or invade us. Fleeing is the only safe action, as Joseph did from Potiphar's wife (Gen 39:12) because he knew that it affected his destiny. Fleeing sexual immorality means avoiding all pornography, fantasy, flirting, even the initial skirmishes which do not seem too significant, but which take us quickly through a door that leads to really big trouble. Every other sin is 'outside' the body (1 Cor 6:18), but sexual sin deeply affects the inside of us in a way that no other sin does.

Fourthly, we are to see to it that no one 'is godless like Esau, who for a single meal sold his birthright.' This is profound. When he was due to inherit the double blessing, the inheritance of the first born, he rejected it. Jacob was cooking lentil stew, when Esau came in famished after being out hunting and asked for some of the stew. Jacob replied, 'first sell me your birthright,' and Esau agreed (Gen 25:29-34). This is an absolutely appalling and shocking moment. Esau was so sensually controlled by his appetites, he gave away the one thing on earth that was most precious to his whole life, the rights of the firstborn. He gave it away in a moment because his appetites outweighed God's promise of inheritance to him.

In Genesis we read of the moment when Abraham realised there was insufficient grazing land for both his and Lot's flocks, so he offered Lot the choice of where to go (Gen 13:8-12). That showed astonishing generosity: the precious land ahead of him, a promise from heaven, and his nephew moving into what he knew was his. So, Lot looked and saw with his natural eyes what he thought would be a great place – Sodom and Gomorrah, in the valley. He was looking with his natural senses, and went to pitch his tents near Sodom, but 'the men of Sodom were wicked, sinning greatly against the Lord' (Gen 13:13). In the end, Lot barely escaped with his life; his wife was less fortunate (Gen 19:15-26). We never want our natural appetites to rule us, and invade the wonder that we are actually the church of the firstborn. The enemy attacks the firstborn, but God blesses them in a remarkable way.

When we make our run of faith well, this releases future generations to make their run of faith even more powerfully. Conversely, Esau did not just lose the birthright for himself, he lost it for subsequent generations as well, and it was never reclaimable. If Esau's descendants ever looked at the promises that were made to Abraham, they would have had to conclude that these would never come to pass for them because of what Esau did. They would think, 'we will never be in the line of inheritance, the promise will never come through our family because of what our grandfather did.' Each of us has been given children to pass on the baton to, and the Lord decides who these children are; it is not just natural children only, but the children he wanted us to affect.

God is revealing here his desire for men and women on his earth to belong, to know their identity. Our natural birthright is a right to a name, to siblings, to a destiny, to lineage and to identity, all given to us at the moment we are born. Similarly, when we are born again, we receive rights, and a lineage with a destiny in heaven's sight. God feels passionately about our heavenly birthright and why he has us on this earth. He does not want our birthright minimised, or questioned, or given away, or lost. God wants to crown us, despite our backgrounds, despite our history, because of who he has made us to be – which we should never despise. And if we keep chasing blessings rather than establishing who we are, we miss out on the foundation of our inheritance. Feeding our appetites or seeking blessings in a moment of need gets in the way of us being established in our identity, rather than having the need met in the short term. Our Father is looking for sons and daughters; we are all firstborn (12:23) and in the new covenant *all* will know him. This is our inheritance, our ultimate purpose, to be conformed to the likeness of Jesus, as we are all sons and daughters of the one Father. We can be assured that God's goodness is not measured by how much blessing we get; he wants so much more for us than just to be receivers of his gifts. He is passionate for our birthright, to have us as firstborn sons and daughters, his image-bearers in the world.

These are the four warnings about areas where we could be weak, and if we don't strengthen these places by doing what we need to get our hearts right, they could end up disabling us. All these situations can potentially incapacitate us in our journey: if there is a gap in relationships that needs addressing, if there are judgments and bitterness towards others, if there is sexual immorality however seemingly innocent, or if there is a kind of godless way inside us that causes us to sacrifice our ultimate calling for the sake of temporary blessing or pleasure.

Chapter 12:18-29

18For you have not come to a mountain that can be touched and that is burning with fire; to darkness, gloom, and storm; 19to a trumpet blast or to a voice that made its hearers beg that no further word be spoken. 20For they could not bear what was commanded: "If even an animal touches the mountain, it must be stoned." 21The sight was so terrifying that even Moses said, "I am trembling with fear."

22Instead, you have come to Mount Zion, to the city of the living God, the heavenly Jerusalem. You have come to myriads of angels 23in joyful assembly, to the congregation of the firstborn, enrolled in heaven. You have come to God the judge of all men, to the spirits of the righteous made perfect, 24to Jesus the mediator of a new covenant, and to the sprinkled blood that speaks a better word than the blood of Abel.

25See to it that you do not refuse Him who speaks. For if the people did not escape when they refused Him who warned them on earth, how much less will we escape if we reject Him who warns us from heaven? 26At that time His voice shook the earth, but now He has promised, "Once more I will shake not only the earth, but heaven as well." 27The words, "Once more," signify the removal of what can be shaken—that is, created things—so that the unshakeable may remain.

28Therefore, since we are receiving an unshakeable kingdom, let us be filled with gratitude, and so worship God acceptably with reverence and awe. 29"For our God is a consuming fire."

12:18-21 The setting is Mount Sinai. What a contrast: today, in these last days he has spoken to us through his Son, and we love every word, but in those days they said 'do not let God speak to us' (Exod 20:19) because they could not bear what was commanded: 'whoever touches the mountain shall surely be put to death' (Exod 19:12). The sight was so terrifying that they all trembled with fear. That is the Old Testament, the external, visible, natural expression of the Old Covenant: terror and awe of a God who is unapproachable. Even Moses, who dealt with God face to face was trembling.

12:22-24 In the New Covenant, however, the unseen realm is opened up to us, as those who come through the blood of Jesus. 'You have come to Mount Zion.' Mount Zion was the place where David installed the ark of the covenant, and where later Solomon built the temple, so this was the earthly dwelling place of God, where all the tribes came together to worship him. Now we have come to the heavenly 'Zion,' where God reigns for ever, and where all come together to worship him in the New Covenant. When did we go there? When we gave our lives to Jesus. This is not 'you will come,' but you *have* come, which is a glorious glimpse of heaven – of all that the heroes of faith in the previous chapter filled their hearts with, of the city of the living God. 'You have come to thousands upon thousands of angels in joyful assembly.' We may wonder what that looks like; Daniel had a vision of myriads upon myriads standing before the Ancient of Days (Dan 7:10) – thousands and thousands of angels are gathered there, with joy flooding all around them. Perhaps we get another glimpse of them at the celebration of the Messiah's birth (Luke 2:13-14).

The 'congregation of the firstborn' is all those who put their trust in Jesus, including us. Everybody in heaven and on earth who has trusted in Jesus and been redeemed by the shedding of his blood has become the church of the firstborn across all heaven and earth, and their names are written in heaven. The blood of Abel was calling out for vengeance, but the blood of Jesus is continually crying out for mercy, for all who come. What we are seeing is the outrageous glory of heaven where all of this is going on, the new Mount Zion, the city of God gloriously coming together, with the spirits of righteous men made perfect by the death and resurrection of Jesus. And we can rejoice that our loved ones who are now in heaven are in this vast company of saints, celebrating and worshipping along with us.

We can develop a very wrong view of heaven, believing perhaps that serious-minded worship continually fills it day and night, or conversely that a reverent awe and silence pervades it. On the contrary, we need to understand the laughter, joy, merriment, and the absolute certainty and assurance that pervades this domain filled with multitudes of angels and saints. Jesus and the Father and the Holy Spirit have the greatest joy of all in the whole cosmos – the Father anointed the Son 'with the oil of joy' (1:9). We need to be clear that joy is a key facet of the activity of this multitude in the courts of heaven, so that when we worship, at our best, we get caught up with all of them.

We are aware that they surround us, cheering us on to our end, because we are all of the same company, 'from whom every family in heaven and on earth derives its name' (Eph 3:15). However we think of it, the unity of those in heaven with those on earth who are following Jesus remains something of a mystery, but somehow we can still see that those who have gone on ahead are not far off. They are in the heavenly realm and are cheering us on and we are with them in the celebration. Heaven's joy should infect us when we start to connect to it in worship – after all, we are all worshipping Jesus together.

12:25-29 Shakings on the earth are a kind of warning and a sign that something is going to happen, an indication that we need to wake up and make sure that our lives are in accord with how God wants them to be, that we are ready. When we see shaking on the earth, whether natural events or political change or 'wars and rumours of wars' (Matt 24:6), we have to hold onto the fact that this is only going to bring an increase of the unshakeable kingdom of God. Shakings do not happen because God is in a bad mood; he is judging the earth, but the shaking will reveal so much more of his kingdom. The result of this is that all who desperately want more of the kingdom can come running into the joy and freedom of a beautiful homecoming. Nebuchadnezzar's dream, interpreted by Daniel, foresaw a time of great turmoil with the overthrow of kingdoms and great shifts in political power. The conclusion was 'the God of heaven will set up a kingdom that will never be destroyed,' and will bring the other kingdoms to an end, 'but will itself stand forever' (Dan 2:44).

'Once more I will shake not only the earth, but heaven as well,' the writer quotes from the prophet Haggai (Hag 2:6). God is not just shaking our planet earth, or even perhaps the rest of the visible universe, but the shaking of all created things includes heaven as well. This is a thorough shaking up of all creation to make way for the new creation, the new order of things that has come about through the resurrection of Jesus, our trailblazer. Our perspective, then, should be that God's kingdom is coming despite the shakings that we see in the world around us, and the purpose of the shaking is always to reveal more of his unshakeable kingdom, the new creation. With a final reference to God as 'a consuming fire' (Deut 4:24), the writer encourages us, in the light of this vision of God's whole end purpose, to worship him 'acceptably with reverence and awe.' This really is the only response we could make, to join with all of heaven and bow in worship before our God – Father, Son and Spirit.

Prayer

Thank you Father that your purpose for us is so great, and you love us so completely, that you sometimes allow circumstances to challenge us profoundly. Give us grace to see these as opportunities for repentance and a deepening in our relationship with you, so that we do not make light of them or lose heart, but grow ever more into our identity as your sons and daughters, in the likeness of Jesus. Amen.

Questions

Can you identify a time when your heavenly Father was disciplining you? If so, what did you learn from that experience?

Is there anybody with whom you do not have complete peace? Is there anybody towards whom you carry some offence or judgment?

Does feeding your appetites limit your higher calling as a son or daughter? What steps can you take to deal with these so that they do not become disabling?

Hebrews 13

Concluding encouragements

Chapter 13:1-8

¹Continue in brotherly love. ²Do not neglect to show hospitality to strangers, for by so doing some people have entertained angels without knowing it. ³Remember those in prison as if you were bound with them, and those who are mistreated as if you were suffering with them.

⁴Marriage should be honoured by all and the marriage bed kept undefiled, for God will judge the sexually immoral and adulterers.

⁵Keep your lives free from the love of money and be content with what you have, for God has said:

> *"Never will I leave you,*
> *never will I forsake you."*

⁶So we say with confidence:

> *"The Lord is my helper; I will not be afraid.*
> *What can man do to me?"*

⁷Remember your leaders who spoke the word of God to you. Consider the outcome of their way of life and imitate their faith. ⁸Jesus Christ is the same yesterday and today and forever.

13:1 The concluding chapter of the book of Hebrews contains encouragements, exhortations, and a little bit of a warning; it is like a very rich postscript to this profound letter. In the first eight verses there are a diverse set of exhortations for the personal life of every believer. The writer focuses in on five different areas of life, but first of all in a beautiful way, verse 1 encourages us to 'continue in brotherly love,' to keep on loving each other as brothers and sisters. This is the anchor or the key for all the other things the writer focuses on. Everything is held together by a commitment in each one of us to keep on loving well, because we are allowing ourselves to be filled by the Father's great love for us. It is the key to everything: if I know I am loved, I can love others. If I am not loved enough, it is hard to keep on loving others in the way that this verse encourages us to do. What a challenge this is!

13:2 The five areas he concentrates on are strangers, those persecuted, marriage, the love of money, and leaders; or we could also say relationships, suffering, sex, money, and power – all the big issues that our contemporary society struggles with every day. The first one is to be hospitable to strangers, because you never know – they could be angels. I've heard many stories of people who have wondered at various moments whether they have met an angel. We had one such experience where one of our sons, who has Down's syndrome, was lost on a huge beach full of crowds of people in the hot sun. We fanned out as a family, desperately trying to find him amidst literally thousands of people, and suddenly a man appeared holding the hand of our son, bringing him towards us, and in that moment of joy at finding him we never quite managed to thank the stranger who then disappeared out of view. I don't know for sure whether this was an angelic presence, but I've heard many stories of similar events.

There are certainly biblical examples to encourage us to show hospitality to strangers. Three men visited Abraham at Mamre, and he welcomed and fed them before they prophesied that Sarah would have a child (Gen 18:1-10). An angel visited Gideon at Ophrah, declaring 'The Lord is with you, mighty warrior.' Gideon only recognised him as an angel when he touched with a staff the food Gideon had prepared and fire flared up to consume it (Judg 6:11-24). Manoah and his wife had a similar experience entertaining a man who prophesied the birth of Samson to them; they realised he was an angel when fire broke out on the sacrifice they had made (Judg 13:1-24). The encouragement to hospitality should provoke a desire in us to have an open heart to every stranger, not necessarily just in our homes but maybe also on the street, out of love for our fellow humans, yes, but also because we never know when we are reaching out to them whether they could be an angel, discovering just how open-hearted we are. Perhaps it could already have happened to us in our journey, when we have reached out to someone to be hospitable, and actually it has been an angel.

13:3 The second area is an encouragement to identify and stand with those believers who are persecuted or in prison. This is a profound issue in our day. Now, in 2019, eleven Christians are killed every day for following Jesus in the fifty countries with the highest levels of persecution. The international ministry Open Doors also estimates that 245 million Christians in the world (1 in 9) experience high levels of persecution, because of their choice to follow Jesus. This is challenging to us because it is not just those being persecuted who suffer; we are encouraged to remember all believers who are suffering through being ill-treated or imprisoned in any way.

What can we do? We want our hearts to be big enough to feel and suffer with our brothers and sisters because we are the same family on earth, just as if our natural brother or sister were in trouble or suffering we would be on the phone to them right away. How much more in God's family do we need to be 'on the phone' in some way, through praying for them, or giving to help alleviate some of the suffering families of those in prison, or even visiting sometimes just to say 'we are with you'? That is huge for those who feel very lonely when they or their relatives are in prison or are really being ill-treated. We need to work out for ourselves what our response should be.

13:4 There is much that could be said about keeping marriage honoured and pure, and this is very challenging in today's culture. Marriage is a divine gift, ordained from the beginning in Genesis 2, for a man and a woman only; there is no other version of marriage. God gave this to us as the most perfect Creator giving a precious gift from the Father, for a man and a woman to share. The purity of sexual union in the marriage bed is at the very centre of this gift, and so we are exhorted to keep it pure, the marriage bed being the place of love-making which not only consummates but also enables that intimate union of marriage to be kept absolutely secure. Any kind of affection or draw elsewhere by one or other in a marriage partnership will spoil that bed, and needs to be repented of and cleansed so that the marriage bed can be pure again.

13:5-6 We all know it is not sinful to have money, it only becomes so when we love it more than we love God, and so the encouragement is to 'keep our lives free from the love of money.' Let us not confuse this. When we love anything to do with money more than we love him, we are making a snare for ourselves, potentially creating an idol; this draws us away from him by making us think 'if only I had more.' Jesus said of the rich young ruler in the gospels that in his case, because of his money, he needed to sell all he had and give to the poor, but he couldn't do it. He didn't want to give away his great wealth, and Jesus didn't try to stop him walking away, but his heart was saddened that this man's wealth had drawn him away from the greatest riches of all (Matt 19:16-22). This doesn't mean that we all have to give away our money; it just means where it has become a snare to us, we need to deal with it. It simply instructs us to be content with what we have.

Contentment is when we are happy that there is sufficient for us because we know the One who provides for us; that is the source of all contentment. However much we have, we don't need to chase more, we don't need to be like an orphan who runs around eagerly trying to find more, because we know our Father in heaven understands what we need and is able to provide it. That is why in the middle of all this encouragement the writer adds references to Deuteronomy 31:6 ('He will never leave you nor forsake you') and Psalm 118:6. All of our contentment is rooted in the Father who says, in his non-abandoning love and provision, 'I will never leave you.' His promise to be our helper is like us being joined to the best and richest provider ever. True confidence and contentment aren't mustered up by our being a bit stronger or richer in ourselves, but they come through a deepening revelation and assurance of who God really is, that gives us the most valuable trust we could ever have.

13:7-8 The last subject of these five is our spiritual leaders, to which the writer will also return again in verse 17. Spiritual abuse that has occurred so much in the church should never detract us from the gift God has provided in those he has called to lead his people in some way. It is a mistake that if we find abuse of a gift, we often turn completely away from the correct use of the gifts God gives. The writer encourages us to look at the way that our leaders have lived, not just at the gift and the anointing that rests on their lives, if we want to find out whether they are his kind of leader. This is a reliable way of knowing who is reflecting God well. If you find a leader whose life is attractive, then imitate their faith: we don't have to imitate their personality, their manner of going about things, their charisma or their style; we are not invited to imitate that. Instead we are invited to imitate their faith that can cause us to live our own faith more deeply.

Then it says that Jesus 'is the same yesterday and today and forever;' in the context of leadership it is saying that Jesus is the ultimate leader, and his consistency to be himself as the firstborn son never changes. It is he who sets the gold standard for every spiritual leader amongst God's people. The old Aaronic priesthood and sacrifices are all over, and there is a new degree of priesthood of all believers, and God's leaders are there to help them come closer to their best.

Chapter 13:9-19

⁹Do not be carried away by all kinds of strange teachings, for it is good for the heart to be strengthened by grace and not by foods of no value to those devoted to them. ¹⁰We have an altar from which those who serve at the tabernacle have no right to eat.

¹¹Although the high priest brings the blood of animals into the Holy Place as a sacrifice for sin, the bodies are burned outside the camp. ¹²And so Jesus also suffered outside the city gate, to sanctify the people by His own blood. ¹³Therefore let us go to Him outside the camp, bearing the disgrace He bore. ¹⁴For here we do not have a permanent city, but we are looking for the city that is to come.

¹⁵Through Jesus, therefore, let us continually offer to God a sacrifice of praise, the fruit of lips that confess His name. ¹⁶And do not neglect to do good and to share with others, for with such sacrifices God is pleased.

¹⁷Obey your leaders and submit to them, for they watch over your souls as those who must give an account. To this end, allow them to lead with joy and not with grief, for that would be of no advantage to you.

¹⁸Pray for us; we are convinced that we have a clear conscience and desire to live honourably in every way. ¹⁹And I especially urge you to pray that I may be restored to you soon.

13:9-13 The writer returns to the central theme of Hebrews: any trust in the Old Covenant and its sacrifices or any legalistic requirements such as food regulations take us back to the wrong altar. This would be Jesus plus something else, rather than Jesus alone, and so the writer is inviting us to go outside the camp, which takes us to the cross, where it has all been paid for. Then we can be strengthened by the promise of the riches of his grace, never again by going to the wrong altar where we would be trying to offer a sacrifice which is of no value because it is obsolete. The blood of Jesus has paid the price for our sin. We are invited to go to the altar of the cross where 'it is finished' releases riches of grace that strengthen our hearts. The free gift of more of Jesus' life and power is available to us when we go to the right altar. The old altar is obsolete; it must never be 'Jesus plus,' just the one altar of the cross.

13:14 This verse returns us to the theme in Hebrews of the tension between this present world, and the heavenly, unseen realm which believers are meant to live from. We are meant to hold this tension right to the end, where ultimately it is fulfilled when Jesus returns, but like Abraham in Hebrews 11, in this life we are all looking for a city that is yet to come. Much of our journey is caught up with having to manage the day-to-day affairs of life, while actually we are aliens on this earth, our citizenship is not on this earth because it is in heaven where there is a city being made ready. We are going to be fully part of this heavenly city but it will only be absolutely fulfilled when Jesus returns; in the meantime we have to live with this tension.

13:15-16 There are two sacrifices mentioned here, the first using language from Hosea 14:2. The sacrifices of the New Covenant are never again blood ones; but the two highlighted here are a stream of praise and doing good to others. These are at the very heart of the message of Jesus (Matt 22:36-40). Praise is a sacrifice because it means we put Jesus as the king-priest at the very centre of our whole lives, all of the time. He can become the centre when through his blood we allow him to replace ourselves on the throne of our lives. We can live with him at the heart of our lives, and this sacrifice leading to praise simply makes him king at the centre of it all.

This releases a constant willingness to share with those who have needs. We have resources, we can give, we can do good and share with others, and these acts of kindness become the outflow of the sacrifice of praise. When we know that God is our all, he is our provision, that he promised never to leave us, and his non-abandoning love runs through our veins, then we can declare, 'because of that satisfying of who I am and of my needs, I can overflow with acts of kindness to others, and that kind of sacrifice you love and are pleased with.' Paul encourages the church in Corinth to, 'see that you also excel in this grace of giving' by describing the most incredible story of the Macedonian churches, who in their poverty have overflowed with generosity because somehow they have engaged with the one provider of all (2 Cor 8:1-8). This illustrates well the sacrifice that our writer is talking about, that grace of giving which is the overflowing of our experience of God being allowed to live at the very centre of our lives.

13:17 We return to the issue of spiritual leaders, our shepherds, and our response to their God-given authority. This is a verse that has been used as a basis for all kinds of leadership abuse, especially where leaders insist on obedience and submission simply because they are in a God-ordained position. This can confuse the genuine believer unless they know they have a freedom to listen to the chief Shepherd's voice as the ultimate leader of their lives. It is a terrible situation where a leader insists on absolute obedience and so violates the freedom of the believer to listen to the voice of Jesus, even while honouring the leader they have been given. Indeed, that kind of violation introduces the first strains of a cult-like society.

This is a really important issue of God adjusting his people to understand how he wants leaders to reflect the chief Shepherd. In this instance, the Greek word for obey – used twice here – is the word *peitho*, which actually means to persuade or win over or have confidence in. This is important because the obedience here is not just by submission to authority, but is the result of being persuaded by someone who reflects God's heart. The word is also closely related to the word *pistis* which means faith or trust. The growing discovery of the Father's true nature through a leader leads us to a trust where our obedience is willing and heartfelt, because we are convinced it is right. This is a process we go through, not a command that we have to obey just because the leader tells us, 'this is what the Lord says.' We come to obey because we have been won over and have developed confidence in what our leaders are asking us to do. With all this in mind, our readiness to respond to true leaders who understand their mandate well makes it more of a joy than a wearisome burden. Why would we want to make things harder for them?

All leadership rests on the twin pillars of protection on the one hand, and empowerment on the other. Overprotection produces control; over-empowerment without protection can produce damage to believers, because they are encouraged to go ahead of what they were ready for. We should all pray that God will bring forth in our day many, many leaders in men and women who really can represent the chief Shepherd well – and not necessarily just those who have been given titles or official roles as leaders within the church.

13:18-19   Having talked about leaders, the writer as a leader himself then asks for prayer for himself. All spiritual leaders need prayer, rather than criticism, or mistrust, or being spoken against. Those who reflect God's heart are doing their very best, so to pray for them is to help them by lifting their arms up – just as Aaron and Hur lifted Moses' arms up, which led to the battle being won by Joshua (Exod 17:11-13). We should do the same for our leaders.

Chapter 13:20-25

20Now may the God of peace, who through the blood of the eternal covenant brought back from the dead our Lord Jesus, that great Shepherd of the sheep, 21equip you with every good thing to do His will. And may He accomplish in us what is pleasing in His sight through Jesus Christ, to whom be glory forever and ever. Amen.

22I urge you, brothers, to bear with my word of exhortation, for I have only written to you briefly.

23Be aware that our brother Timothy has been released. If he arrives soon, I will come with him to see you.

24Greet all your leaders and all the saints.

Those from Italy send you greetings.

25Grace be with all of you.

13:20-21 This is a glorious apostolic prayer for the readers of this letter, and for the writer himself, summing up so much of what he has explained in detail. He prays that God would give us everything we need in order to do his will, and that God would accomplish in us what he wants to do. It is about what we do in the world in following God's ways, but it is also a prayer that God will form us into the people he created us to be. He is interested both in empowering the daily living of our lives well, but also in establishing our identities as his beloved sons and daughters after the likeness of his Son. This is all done through Jesus, the great and glorious Shepherd of us all – a powerful theme of the bible from Psalm 23 onwards. Everything about our lives and our provision must always come back to the centre of his deep and unfailing love for us, as 'that great Shepherd of the sheep.'

13:22-25 In these concluding words, we are reminded that the whole letter has been an unending call for us to finish the race strongly, and always through God's wonderful grace. I hope and trust that every one of us will know that grace resting powerfully on us throughout our lives, until we hear his great 'welcome home' for us, his sons and daughters, who finished the race well. May we all finish well, and may this letter help us do so.

Prayer

Father, we thank you for the privilege of journeying with you through this letter to the Hebrews. We thank you that your desire is always to bring many sons to glory, for us to encounter your fathering love and so be transformed increasingly into the likeness of your Son. We ask you, God of grace, to show us daily more of who you are as our Father, and to equip us with every good thing we need in order to live more and more as your sons and daughters, so that as we run life's marathon we might faithfully reflect your glorious nature to the world around us. Amen.

Questions

What have you learned from your journey through the letter to the Hebrews? What has encouraged you the most? What has challenged you?

What steps can you take in order to follow the writer's command to 'continue in brotherly love'? What might this look like in practice in your own daily life?

Printed in Poland
by Amazon Fulfillment
Poland Sp. z o.o., Wrocław

49027329R00121